Los Mojados: The Wetback Story

Los Mojados: The Wetback Story

**by
Julian Samora**

with the assistance of
JORGE A. BUSTAMANTE F.
and GILBERT CARDENAS

UNIVERSITY OF NOTRE DAME PRESS
NOTRE DAME   LONDON

To those valiant men, women, and children whose suffering
is so much a part of our affluence.

This study was produced through the U.S.-Mexico Border Studies Project at the University of Notre Dame, under the direction of Julian Samora, sponsored by a grant from the Ford Foundation. The opinions expressed in the report do not necessarily represent the views of the Foundation.

Contents

Acknowledgments

The writing of a book is never the work of only one person. I am indebted to many people most of whom cannot be mentioned by name.

Dr. S. M. Miller, Mrs. Siobhan Oppenheimer, and Mr. Mike Sviridoff of The Ford Foundation, together with Mr. Paul Ylavasaker, formerly of The Ford Foundation, were most instrumental in the provision of funds for this and other research.

Mr. James F. Greene, Associate Commissioner of Immigration and Naturalization Service, made much data available and opened many doors at regional and local offices. Officials of the Border Patrol, together with officials of the holding and detention centers at San Ysidro, El Centro, El Paso, and Los Fresnos, were most cooperative throughout the research. The participant-observation study reported in the next to the last chapter was conducted with the knowledge and approval of the Immigration and Naturalization Service. We thank them for the legal protection provided the observer, our "wetback," Mr. Bustamante. Using a false name he played the role so well that we never had to call upon the Immigration Service for the help they so graciously offered. His experience remains embedded in his memory and untold bureaucratic records.

My graduate students, Jorge A. Bustamante and Gilbert Cardenas, were particularly helpful in the details of this report. Dr. Ernesto Galarza and Dr. John Price offered many helpful suggestions in an early version of the manuscript.

The photographs came to us through the courtesy of the U.S. Border Patrol, the Amalgamated Meat Cutters and Butcher Workmen of North America/AFL-CIO, and the Texas Labor Archives of the University of Texas at Arlington.

Miss Guadalupe Solis and Mrs. Elaine McKenzie shared the burden of endless typing.

The staff of the University of Notre Dame Press, in particular Miss Ann Rice, "put us all together," in the final analysis.

My family put up with *Los Mojados* and made the wetback story possible.

Introduction

In the late afternoon of September 29, 1968, forty-six Mexican male aliens walked to a designated point about one mile upriver from the international bridge near Piedras Negras, Mexico. They waited until 3:00 A.M. when a Mexican guided them across the river afoot and led them upriver on the American side for about two hours. The man who guided them collected fifty dollars from most of them and told them to wait in the gully until they would be picked up later in the morning. He then departed, presumably returning to Mexico.

At about 11:00 A.M. on September 30, 1968, another man appeared and told them that they would be picked up in about an hour. When he returned, he collected fifty dollars from each and told them to come out of the gully. They entered a U-Haul truck waiting on the bank. The entire group had the intention of going to Chicago, Illinois, to work.

Among them were Mr. Garcia, forty years of age, from Moroleón, Guanajuato, Mexico, who was married and had eight children; Mr. Lopez, eighteen years old and also from Moroleón; Mr. Guzman, thirty-eight years old, from Uitzio, Michoacán, Mexico, married and seven children; Mr. Vieyra, thirty-nine years old, from Uridia, Guanajuato, Mexico, married and seven children; Mr. Diaz, thirty-nine years old, from Michoacán, married and eight children.

After they had entered the truck they were locked in. They never saw the driver of the truck. Upon arrival in Chicago they were to pay another hundred dollars.

None of the men had been contacted in their respective

communities, but it was common knowledge in their community (according to their testimony) that if one took a bus to Piedras Negras and stayed at a particular hotel, he would be contacted and for $200 he could get to Chicago. This is precisely what these men did.

En route some men began to faint for lack of air, others to gasp for breath, others yelled and pounded on the walls of the truck. The driver stopped the truck and told them that he could not open the doors because he did not have a key but that they were only thirty minutes away from San Antonio, Texas.

Upon arrival at San Antonio at a particular address, one or two of the aliens, in a dazed condition, got out and walked into the neighboring yard. Two or three tried to hide in the alley behind the garage.

The neighbors called the police about a disturbance at this address, and the police arrived at about 4:30 P.M. The police were assured by the person who answered the door that there was no disturbance at this address. Twenty minutes later another call of a disturbance was received by the police. This call was also answered by the police, but in the meantime the smugglers had escaped. A search revealed some of the aliens hiding in the house, some in the truck, some in the garage, and others in the neighbor's yard. Ambulances and more police cars were called, and the Immigration Service was advised.

Thirteen of the Mexicans were taken to a local hospital. One was dead on arrival and two others died the following day. Of the forty-six aliens, twenty-three were returned to Mexico, three had died, and twenty were held as witnesses to this case and farmed out for work in San Antonio.

The three smugglers who were caught a few days later were indicted by the grand jury in Del Rio, Texas, October 22, 1968, on twenty-four counts of conspiracy and transportation of aliens. Their bond was set at $15,000 each and a bench warrant was issued for their arrest. They appeared with their attorneys in San Antonio on October 24, 1968, and made bond. The leader of the smuggling operation was indicted on three other smuggling counts filed by the Del Rio Immigration Office. He made bond of $5,000 in each of the three cases. Juan T. Eguia, the leader of the three, received a sentence totaling thirty-eight years, of which he is to serve twenty-three years. Carlos Becerra received a sentence totaling twenty years, of which he is to serve ten years. Joe Roy Campos was given ten years to serve.

Incidents like the above are reported daily throughout the United States. In 1969, 2,048 smugglers were apprehended, their transactions involving thousands of aliens. This figure was almost four times the number of smugglers (525) apprehended in 1965. As of June 1, 1970, with one more month left in the fiscal year, over 3,000 smugglers had been apprehended. (See Appendix I, Question 25.)

The smuggling of human bodies is greatly on the increase, but it is only a small part of the drama of illegal entry into the United States from Mexico, which involves thousands of persons whose stories seldom have a happy ending.

All nation states regulate the movement of foreign persons and goods across their borders. The regulations reflect the value orientations, the deeply held beliefs, as well as the prejudices prevalent within the society.

The entry of illegal aliens into a country has always been of great concern to the government in question. In the case of the United States, the Immigration and Naturalization Service has historically devoted most of its efforts to the control of illegal entrants. In recent years the overwhelming majority of illegal entrants into the United States have been from Mexico.

The study of illegal aliens has not captured the imagination of American social scientists, as have other topics. Moreover, while researching the subject of Mexican illegal aliens, it soon became clear that there was a dearth of information available on this subject, in spite of the apparent import of the problem, replete with national and international implications. There are, to the writer's knowledge, only two books on the subject. Serious and scholarly writings are not many and have appeared only now and again. Even the professors in the many U.S. universities located in "the border region," the four states bordering Mexico, have seldom bothered to direct their graduate students to exploit this potentially rich field of inquiry.

Significance of the Study

Of the myriad topics available for study in the border region, we chose to study the Mexican illegal alien for a number of reasons. In this volume we present only a guide and an outline of the problem; we hope that this work will stimulate many other scholars to enter this field of inquiry.

The illegal movement of hundreds of thousands of people from one country to another in itself is atypical. Few nations have ever witnessed or experienced such a phenomenon, short of conquest. The consequences to Mexico and to the United States of this mass movement are many and provide the rationale for this study.

What does it mean to Mexico to have thousands of its citizens crossing illegally into the United States year after year? It means that many people are uprooted and displaced. Small communities within Mexico are disrupted, as people move from rural areas to urban areas and to the northern border. Cities, and particularly those on the northern border, are overrun with the new migrants. A multitude of social problems is created, including problems of health, delinquency and crime, poverty, unemployment, welfare, and the break-up of family units. Mexican cities which are invaded by these migrants have difficulty in supplying housing, utilities, medical and welfare services, police protection, and employment. The schools in these cities obviously cannot absorb a great influx of children, nor can teachers and classrooms be provided.

To the extent that Mexican illegal aliens are successful in entering and remaining in the United States and finding employment, the Mexican economy gains in two ways: Persons are employed who would otherwise be a burden in their country, and money is sent to Mexico from the United States by persons who would otherwise be unemployed.

The individual alien himself has the strange experience of leaving his family, friends, community, and country for an undetermined period of time. He lives outside of the law, on the fringes of society, in constant fear of being apprehended. Invariably he leads a life of hardship, and he is at the mercy of those who would exploit him.

For the United States the entrance of thousands of illegal aliens every year has many consequences. In the first place it is costly. The annual budget for the Immigration and Naturalization Service in 1969 was $89,699,300 (U.S. Department of Justice, The Judiciary, 1969:584). This included support for the Border Patrol, which involves the services of several hundred officials and the maintenance of many offices, a training center, hundreds of vehicles including airplanes and boats, and the costs of transporting aliens within the U.S. and abroad. The maintenance of one holding station in San Ysidro, California, and three detention centers located at El Centro, California; El Paso, Texas, and Los Fresnos, Texas, is also included in the budget. Each of the detention centers has 100 to 300 aliens on any given day. Many are held from one to two weeks pending investigation of their cases if felonies or crimes are suspected or if deportation action is involved. Most aliens in detention centers who express a desire for voluntary departure and who, aside from their illegal entry, are not suspected of having violated any laws are processed within a day or two and expelled from the country. But it is expensive to process, house, feed, and transport several hundred aliens every day.

In addition to the expenditures of the Immigration and Naturalization Service, there are court costs, the cost of parole and probation, incarceration in federal prisons, and the work of other agencies within the Justice Department and in other departments such as those of State, Agriculture, Commerce, the Treasury, and the Interior.

To the U.S. economy the entry of illegal aliens is profitable in at least three ways: the employment of officials to apprehend, care for, and expel the aliens; the money that the aliens spend before being apprehended; and the cheap labor which the aliens represent.

In the United States, organized labor views the aliens as both a threat and an obstacle: a threat in the sense that they will work for whatever wage is offered and will even be strikebreakers, and an obstacle in that the aliens hinder unionization and collective bargaining efforts.

U.S. citizens who live in the border region and who lack sophisticated employment skills look upon the aliens as a threat because they will work for less and they are a readily available source of labor. Mexican-American citizens and Mexican citizens who are legal resident aliens in the United States often have to compete with the illegal alien for the unskilled employment available in the border region. This is true in agriculture, in many industries, in service employment, and in domestic employment.

The illegal entry of such large numbers of persons creates a series of problems in communities where they live. Housing is perhaps the most critical of these. The illegal alien has few choices as to where he will live and how much rent he will pay. The most primitive of accommodations are not unusual for these individuals, particularly those who work in agriculture. Since the great majority of the aliens are men and in the younger age group, problems characteristic of homeless men are common to them: prostitution, venereal disease, drunkenness, delinquency, and crime. Mexican and United States agencies working in public health, welfare, police protection, narcotics, and many other fields have for years made joint efforts to solve these social problems. Many agencies have organized into border conferences and hold yearly meetings.

Persons who employ illegal aliens at less than minimum wages profit enormously from such labor. Since illegal aliens have no rights within the law and since they can be turned in to the authorities so easily, some employers take advantage of this situation and don't pay the aliens before turning them in. Other employers, particularly in industry in the North, hire aliens at union wages.

Persons who traffic in human beings, the smugglers, have made the most profit from the illegal alien. Smuggling has been a most lucrative business. The price for smuggling individuals has been high, the costs have been relatively low, and the penalties if caught, until very recently, have been minimal and evidently well worth the risk.

Wetbacks, Alambristas

Certain categories of persons will be discussed throughout the volume. Our main concern is with the illegal Mexican alien, whom we will label through common usage the *wetback*. This appellation has been used since the 1920's to designate those persons who have crossed the Rio Grande from Mexico in order to enter the United States without legal inspection. Those who have illegally crossed the international border where no river exists—between San Diego, California, and El Paso, Texas—are also popularly known as wetbacks, but they may have cut a fence in order to cross, and therefore the term *alambrista* may be used for this particular group.

Braceros

We will also talk about temporary contract seasonal farm workers supplied by various nations. Those farm laborers who have come from Mexico have been called *braceros*. They came from Mexico under an international agreement between Mexico and the United States, whereby Mexico was to supply temporary farm workers to help in the war effort during the last world war.

Commuters

The commuter, so labeled on the United States-Mexico border, is basically a person from Mexico who has acquired an immigrant visa, Form I-151, which entitles him to *reside* and work in the U.S. as a legal resident alien. This type of documentation is in reality a bona fide immigrant visa, but because of history, custom, and tradition, the immigration and residence stipulations have become obscure and the visa has become a work permit. This is to say that Mexicans with an immigrant visa, Form I-151 (often called *green-carders*), live in Mexico and commute to the United States to work.

Commuters, however, are not all Mexican citizens; there are many commuters on the Canadian-United States border. Some commuters are United States citizens, born in the United States of Mexican parents, but who have lived in Mexico most of their lives and have obtained work in the United States.

Border Crossers

Other "commuters" are not legal alien residents (Form I-151) but persons who have a border-crossing permit, Form I-186, which entitles them to come across for visiting, shopping, business, and pleasure, for a period not to exceed seventy-two hours. Many persons holding these border-crossing cards do in fact cross the border legally into the United States but violate the law by working in the United States (for example, as domestics), contrary to the regulations upon which the permit is issued.

Many wetbacks, particularly in the lower Rio Grande valley in Texas, are also commuters. They commute daily, and illegally, to work in Texas farm fields when seasonal farm work is available.

Why Wetbacks?

Mexican illegal aliens have been apprehended in almost every state of the Union and in most large cities. Thirty-eight were arrested on the Alaska Railroad close to the Arctic Circle in 1951 (Hadley, 1956:336). In 1964, 1,114 Mexican aliens were apprehended in Chicago. Four were apprehended in 1965 in San Juan, Puerto Rico. In 1966, nine were apprehended in Honolulu. The number of apprehensions for 1968 was 151,680 Mexicans, of whom 18,681 were women and children; and in 1969 of 283,557 aliens apprehended, 201,636 were Mexicans (U.S. Department of Justice, I & N Annual Reports).

The largest number of illegal Mexican aliens ever apprehended in one year, as reported by the Department of Justice, was 1,075,168, in 1954. Shortly thereafter "Operation Wetback" was initiated. This intensive attempt to control the illegal movement of people across the Mexico-U.S. border was quite successful. The decline in the apprehensions in the years that followed was most significant and the situation appeared to be contained. The enforcement of the law was so thorough that one researcher was prompted to say:

> With Attorney General Brownell, who was willing to give real support to enforcement of immigration law on our southern border, with General Swing's leadership, and with budget increases, the day of the wetback is over. The border should be under control by the end of 1956. This job, considered hopeless by many, will have been accomplished in two years. [Hadley, 1956:351]

It must be remembered that at the time of the above report the legal arrangement for the importation of Mexican temporary seasonal farm workers between Mexico and the United States was still in effect. This program, usually called the Bracero Program, brought over four million workers from Mexico to the United States between 1942 and 1964. Begun as a wartime (World War II) measure, it was renewed time and again in spite of great opposition to it from many quarters. The powerful farm lobbies were successful in keeping the program alive through December of 1964.

A look at the illegal movement of people across the Mexican border, which was supposed to be under control by 1956, reveals, however, that there has been a steady increase from 1964 to the present time. Some persons, including officials of the Immigration and Naturalization Service, have suggested that the increase in wetbacks is due to the elimination of the Bracero Program. There is some truth in this, but only up to a point. We have to remember that even in 1954, when the Bracero Program was in full swing, over a million wetbacks were apprehended—the highest figure in history. Other reasons for the increase in the illegal traffic are suggested.

The two most compelling reasons for illegal immigration are the insatiable demand for cheap labor in the United States and the tremendous population increase occurring in Mexico. Mexico's population growth rate is among the highest in the world. Although Mexico's economic growth programs have made enormous strides, the economy has not been able to provide sufficient employment, schools, income, and services for the increasing population. While its food production is high, the availability of food for the poor is a problem not unlike that of underdeveloped and the developing countries. As a matter of fact, similar problems of distribution plague the United States, a "developed" country.

United States agriculture and agribusiness owes its success to two well-known factors: the exploitation of cheap labor and government subsidies. This sector of the economy has been exempt from legislation favorable to and protective of workers. One hundred years ago, when agricultural production was mostly a family affair, this special treatment might have made sense. Today, when agriculture is admittedly an industry, the labor supplying this industry has only recently even been able to bargain collectively.

As agribusiness becomes larger, the situation encourages a great demand for a cheap and mobile labor force. The Bracero Program was just such a labor force and, besides that, it was partially subsidized by the federal government. Wetback labor is even cheaper—no need for contracts, minimum wage, health benefits, housing, transportation, etc. Since the workers are illegal aliens, they have few rights before the law and can be dismissed at a moment's notice.

The internal migrations taking place in Mexico are another factor influencing the illegal traffic into the United States. The rural to urban population movements in Mexico seem to have as their ultimate destinations two urban areas: Mexico City and the cities along the Mexico-U.S. border. The northern border has always been a great magnet for Mexico's internal population movements. The four largest *municipios* (similar to counties) have had fantastic population increases in the past thirty years and attest to this fact:

Municipio	1940	1967
Tijuana	21,977	347,501
Mexicali	44,399	540,300
Ciudad Juárez	55,024	501,416
Nuevo Laredo	31,502	140,818

Attracted by the stories of work opportunities in the United States, the poor of Mexico have been piling up along the border in the hope of entering the United States, either legally or illegally.

Any city in any country growing at such a phenomenal rate would be hard put to provide adequate housing, utilities, welfare and medical service, schools, churches, police protection, and employment. The pressures building up on the Mexican side of the border tend to be relieved through illegal entry into the United States.

This situation creates high unemployment on the Mexican side of the border as well as a great labor pool for the United States side, which vies legally (commuters) or illegally (wetbacks) with United States labor for the available jobs in the U.S. border region and elsewhere. The end result of this competition appears to be a depressing of the wage structure (except where unionization has been successful) and the displacement of United States labor (especially Mexican-Americans). This displaced domestic agricultural labor has entered the agricultural migrant stream in great numbers, and is pushed farther and farther away from home base. Over the years this process has produced enclaves of Mexican-American settlements throughout the United States, as the Mexican-Americans have dropped out of the migrant stream at every opportunity of a steady job, a decent wage, and an education for their children. In many northern places they have joined small groups of Chicanos who ventured into this area starting in the 1920's and '30's.

A last reason for the increase in the wetback movement is the fact that there are no great penalties involved in being a wetback, *nor in hiring a wetback.* Both parties, employer and employee, can happily break the law time and time again, the only serious consequence being an inconvenience to one or another or both. (See Appendix I; 48, 49.)

The Presentation

The above sketch sets the stage for the wetback story. Chapter I will review some of the literature and give the historical background of the border region so that the wetback story can be placed in perspective and be better understood. The controversial Bracero Program which left a permanent imprint on the peoples of both nations will be summarized, and the commuter situation, the subject of the recent (1969 and 1970) congressional hearing and current legislation, will be analyzed.

A short history of illegal Mexican immigration into the United States will be given in Chapter II.

The difficulties encountered in interviewing wetbacks north of the border, in such states as Illinois and Indiana, will be discussed in Chapter III. This chapter will also discuss the methodological problems encountered in this study.

Much of what happens to illegal aliens in the United States upon being apprehended resembles a game rather than a serious violation of the law with international consequences. In Chapter IV we try to explain how the arrangements are made, the contacts necessary for crossing the border, and how documents are obtained. We shall also attempt to show how one gets across the border.

Chapter V will concentrate on the range and extent of the illegal movement. It will also specify the type of employment, wages earned, the length of time the men spent in the United States, and the number of times they were caught and where.

It is the contention of this work that Mexicans in general and wetbacks in particular view the United States with a degree of misguided awe with regard to its affluence, political power, employment opportunities, high wages, justice, freedom, and equality. Many build up great expectations of enjoying such a utopia, only to discover that "it ain't necessarily so." Chapter VI presents a profile of the wetback and the reasons why he plays the game. It also attempts to reveal the reality of the conditions encountered in the new situation, the problems of living outside of the society while working within it, and the uncertainty of illegal alien status. The exploitation which occurs at all levels is examined.

What it feels like to be a wetback—to cross over by night and walk or crawl through planted fields and snake-infested brush, always dodging strangers, dogs, and especially *la migra* (the Border Patrol)—why you do this, and what becomes of you are made immediately real in the unusual account which is Chapter VII. The "wetback" here is one of our researchers using one more sociologists' tool, participant observation, to add to our store of information and verify information already gathered. But the equally valuable byproducts of his venture were the personal insights drawn from the comradeship he found and the situations encountered. They bring into sharp focus many of the human reasons for undertaking this study.

The final chapter will deal with a number of questions of national and international interest. It will examine the stakes involved for the respective governments in perpetuating this system. It will look to see who profits from this exploitation and will suggest development of realistic national policies which may benefit the poor of both nations.

The editorial "we" is used throughout the book. Although Jorge A. Bustamante F. and Gilbert Cardenas gave invaluable assistance in this research, the opinions expressed are those of the author.

i: *The Border Region*

The border region is labeled so only because there is an imaginary line separating two political entities, not because of any cultural, physical, geographical, or natural phenomena which make the territory distinctive and distinguishable.

The boundary line begins at the Pacific Ocean about fifteen miles south of San Diego and extends beyond Brownsville, Texas, to the Gulf of Mexico.

Between the Pacific Ocean and El Paso, Texas, the terrain on both sides of the line is largely harsh, rocky country or desert land. The boundary line between these two points crosses the states of California, Arizona, and New Mexico. With few exceptions (where water is available), agricultural, mining, and industrial endeavors along the border are all small enterprises. The one major exception is the great agricultural development of the Imperial Valley on the California side of the boundary.

As the line enters Texas, moving east toward the Gulf of Mexico it crosses a few low mountains. El Paso was established here years before there was any boundary. El Paso came to be the gateway to the north or *El Paso del Norte*. This area became the main crossing point for those Spaniards, Indians, and, later, Mexicans who moved from southern Mexico to the northern territory or the Spanish borderlands, which encompassed much of what is now the southwestern United States.

At El Paso the Río Bravo or the Rio Grande becomes the international political boundary between the two nations. The river, which originates in the high mountains of Colorado, moves southward as it flows past El Paso. As it follows the rugged terrain and moves through Big Bend National Park it continues on a southeasterly course and eventually empties into the Gulf of Mexico.

Between Big Bend National Park and the Gulf of Mexico the terrain becomes semitropical and irrigated agriculture predominates. On the U.S. side of the boundary the area becomes known as the lower Rio Grande valley.

There are few bridges which cross the approximately nine hundred miles of river between El Paso and Brownsville, and these are only between twin cities. In the land expanse from El Paso west to the ocean there are few roads which cross the boundary and these again are between twin cities. No roads or railroads parallel the border from one end to the other on either side of the boundary.

Professor Fred Schmidt (Schmidt, 1970) suggests an "oasis society" as a description of the social development along the boundary line. Wherever twin cities occur on the border, they evidently service large geographical areas and great populations on either side of the boundary.

Beginning in California we find on the border Tijuana, in Baja California, and San Ysidro, in California. Fifteen miles north of San Ysidro is San Diego and 120 miles north of that is Los Angeles, the city with the greatest concentration of Mexican-Americans in the U.S. Only two cities have a greater concentration of persons of Mexican descent than Los Angeles: Mexico City and Guadalajara. Tijuana has increased in population over 1000 percent between 1940 and 1967, making it one of the fastest growing cities in the world.

A few miles east, also in Baja California is Mexicali, another of the fastest growing cities in the world. Across the border is Calexico, the gateway to the Imperial Valley, one of the richest agricultural areas in the U.S. Much of the agricultural labor for the Imperial Valley has been supplied by Mexicans from Mexicali.

In Arizona three twin cities have developed: San Luis, Nogales, and Agua Prieta in Sonora and San Luis, Nogales, and Douglas in Arizona. North of these Arizona border towns are Tucson and Phoenix.

New Mexico has only one small town on the border, Columbus, and its twin town is Palomas, Chihuahua.

El Paso begins the twin cities in Texas. Juárez, Chihuahua is across the border. El Paso is less than one-half million in population; Juárez is slightly over half a million, the largest Mexican border city along with Tijuana and Mexicali. The remaining twin cities are: Villa Acuña–Del Rio; Piedras Negras–Eagle Pass; Nuevo Laredo–Laredo; Reynosa–McAllen, and Matamoros–Brownsville.

Well over one hundred million crossings of U.S. and Mexican citizens are recorded each year by the inspection stations on this border, giving evidence to the volume of intercourse between the two nations.

In the beginning there was no international boundary in this region. Indians roamed the area and some settled temporarily or permanently along the rivers. The Spaniards, who came much later, also used the rivers, in particular the Rio Grande, as they divested the inhabitants of their lands, in the name of God and country. The borderlands were important to Spain for settlement. They represented the outpost and the frontier of Spanish settlement in North America, with its center in Mexico City.

The borderlands so far from Spain, Cuba, and Mexico City, came to serve as a great buffer between New Spain and foreign powers such as England, France, the United States, and Russia. The English, the French, and the Russian threats to this area were eventually contained or came to naught. But the encroachment of the United States finally reached to the Pacific Ocean and gobbled up both land and people in the process. As Spain declined as a world power, her colonies revolted and established new nations. Mexico became one of these new nations, establishing her independence by 1823.

Spain lost most of its New World possessions in the first quarter of the nineteenth century. The territory which became Mexico encompassed an area from the Pacific Ocean to the Gulf of Mexico and from Guatemala north to include the present U.S. border states (California, Arizona, New Mexico, and Texas), and all or parts of Nevada, Utah, and Colorado.

Mexico, hoping to maintain this vast, sparsely populated area but unable to defend it militarily, followed a course which it was later to regret: It permitted foreigners to colonize the borderlands (particularly Texas) in an effort to populate part of the region and stave off foreign encroachment. The conditions under which settlement was to be permitted were quite explicit, including the regulation that settlers must become citizens of Mexico and uphold the law and religion of the land. The stipulations, however, were generally ignored, and U.S. citizens largely commandeered much of the region and pushed ever westward. Seen in retrospect, Mexico's course of action was much like letting the cat get into the bird cage. There usually isn't much left of the bird.

Meanwhile the United States pursued what it considered to be its manifest destiny, to own and control the vast land area from the eastern seaboard to the Pacific Ocean. As the frontier approached the Southwest and as more and more Americans came into Texas, it was no secret that the U.S., under President Jackson, on several occasions sent an envoy to Mexico City to press for the purchase of Texas to the Rio Grande. Five million dollars was offered, but without success. (See Horgan, 1954:513.)

It took "Texans" approximately thirteen years to acquire their territory from Mexico and set up a republic. It took the U.S. another twelve years to acquire the rest of the territory to the Pacific Ocean and to annex Texas, which was populated by its own former citizens! To accomplish all of these real estate transactions the United States used a variety of methods, including an unjust war. The history of the period shows without question the blatant determination of the U.S. to acquire this territory.

When the formalities were over, the treaty (Guadalupe Hidalgo) signed, the money exchanged, indemnities paid, the troops removed, and the boundary established, a considerable number of people found themselves with new citizenship, which in reality (despite the treaty and the constitution) did not mean much to the conquered people. Their status was not changed appreciably, until later when they were separated from their land.

The Indians were soon placed on reservations, a solution whose consequences continue to plague the nation today. The Spanish-speaking were largely ignored, while the nation set out to "develop" the land. Most of the land had been acquired through conquest, a small portion was bought. That land which was public domain was available for transfer and "development"; that which belonged to individuals had to be taken from them, and soon was. Thus the Americans divested the Mexican-American of his land and began to develop agriculture, mining, railroads, and industry which now rival their counterparts in other regions.

When the United States came into possession of this territory, it is estimated that people with Spanish-surnames numbered 100,000 (Saunders, 1950). History books do not tell us what happened to this population between 1850 and 1920. It is fairly certain that those persons who lived in isolated villages in northern New Mexico and southern Colorado were largely geographically isolated and were ignored by the federal government. They were also bypassed by the development of the Southwest and then were "discovered" in the 1940's. We can only guess that those Mexican-Americans who lived in other areas supplied the labor for the developing region and were left to form their own ghettos, which are still evident today in all major cities. With few exceptions every town and city in the Southwest has its Mexican-American section, suggesting a long-established practice of segregation in housing, employment, and education.

As early as 1911, Mexican immigration had aroused enough concern as to be the subject of study by the Dillingham Commission, which reported on immigration into the United States and made recommendations on the basis of its findings. That commission reported:

> Because of their strong attachment to their native land, low intelligence, illiteracy, migratory life, and the possibility of their residence here being discontinued, few become citizens of the United States. . . . In so far as Mexican laborers come into contact with natives or with European immigrants they are looked upon as inferiors. . . . Thus it is evident that in the case of the Mexican he is less desirable as a citizen than as a laborer. [Dillingham Commission, vol. I, 1911:690–691].

As to the border region, people have moved back and forth across the border without much interruption, with Mexicans supplying the labor for the region. The region grew in Mexican population, but no one knows how much. No records were kept of Mexican immigration between 1886 and 1893. Speaking of the period before 1910, Professor Leo Grebler says:

> Literature ranging from historical treaties to folklore testifies
> to substantial movements of people across the Mexican border
> long before such movements were controlled, classified, and mea-
> sured. In fact, one of the early mass migrations occurred just as
> the southwest territories were annexed to the United States; large
> numbers of Sonorans and others joined in the trek to the Califor-
> nia gold rush. Shepherds, cowboys and farm workers crossed the
> border in both directions as if there were no boundary. [Grebler,
> 1965:19]

The Revolution of 1910 in Mexico pushed many Mexicans
out of their country and into the United States.

The First World War, with the expansion of defense industries and the drafting of United States citizens (including
many Mexican-Americans) created a large labor shortage. To
a great extent the U.S. labor force was replenished by Mexicans. When the 1924 National Origins Act greatly diminished
immigration from Europe and other parts of the world, Mexico,
again, was the great supplier of labor.

> World War II virtually eliminated immigration. Existing farm
> labor went into military service or higher paying industry jobs,
> leaving the agricultural labor market in the Southwest to the
> Spanish-speaking population, who could not qualify for war in-
> dustry because of language difficulty, discrimination, lack of skills,
> or lack of citizenship. The Bracero Agreement of 1942 with
> Mexico and the "wetback" took up most of the labor shortage.
> [William E. Scholes in Samora, 1966:66]

The Bracero Program

The bilateral government agreement for the recruitment of
agricultural labor was first conceived as a war emergency
measure. It lasted, however, for twenty-two years, or until 1964.

As agriculture became commercial, it depended on seasonal
farm labor in great numbers and out of proportion to the year-
around work force (Galarza, 1964). At first this labor was supplied haphazardly, mostly from Mexico. The flow of workers
from across the border continued at an ever-increasing pace, in
what has been called "migration by drift" (Galarza, 1964).
This migration accounted for a tremendous increase of population in the Mexican cities on the border as well as for over a
million and a half Mexican entrants (illegal and legal) into the

United States before 1940, supplying a vast labor pool. This pool was managed through the establishment of farm placement services in the state departments of employment and through the growth of labor-recruiting associations. It goes without saying that the growers set the wages, managed the labor supply, encouraged an oversupply of labor, and, with the help of the law-enforcing officers, suppressed any attempts at strikes.

The Second World War absorbed so much manpower in both the armed services and defense industries that a labor crisis was said to exist. Again the place to turn to was Mexico. With the help of both governments the employers of farm labor were given an ideal situation: It was a labor program that was planned, inexpensive, efficient, administered to benefit the employer, and mostly subsidized by the United States government. This was the birth of the Bracero Program in 1942. It is not our purpose to detail the history of the Bracero Program; this has been done elsewhere (Galarza, 1964). Rather, we wish to indicate the magnitude of the program in the number of persons attracted to it and admitted into the United States, and to examine the relationship of this to our main topic, the wetback.

As stated earlier, the Bracero Program began as a war emergency measure and it was amended as well as violated several times. After the war, the State Department notified Mexico in 1946 that it wished to terminate the agreement within ninety days. The agricultural interests, however, succeeded in having the agreement extended until 1951, and in that year Congress was persuaded to enact Public Law 78, which remained in effect until the end of 1964! Between 1942 and 1950 over 430,000 braceros entered the United States. This was at least four years beyond the war emergency. Between 1951 and 1964, Under Public Law 78, 4,336,785 braceros entered the United States. Thus, during the twenty-two year period of its existence approximately 4.8 million braceros were contracted. During the same time period over 5 million wetbacks were apprehended. We are speaking, then, of a population statistic of 10 million. If each statistic represented a separate individual, this would represent a sizable portion of the population of Mexico. We know, however, that an individual bracero may have been chosen in five different years and therefore is counted here five times, or a wetback may have been apprehended from one to twenty times and counted each time he was apprehended. Nevertheless, for any given year the number of Mexicans who entered the country, legally or illegally, was sizable, as shown in the tables which follow.

Commuters°

At five o'clock in the morning at the international bridge between El Paso and Ciudad Juárez a trickle of humanity begins the daily trek from Mexico to the U.S. By 8:00 A.M. the trickle has become a torrent and thousands of people have crossed into El Paso. To a greater or lesser degree, the same situation is evident at all the border crossing points: Tijuana, Mexicali, Nogales, Piedras Negras, Nuevo Laredo, Reynosa, and Matamoros.

Professor Leo Grebler (1965:63), using data from Mexico's Programa Nacional Fronterizo, gives a minimum estimate of 60,000 commuters for 1960. Data on commuters is woefully inadequate because these data are not compiled systematically. There is no record of the actual number of persons who have a "green card" (Form I-151) which permits individuals to work in the United States and live either in Mexico or the U.S. Thus holders of the green card may commute daily or periodically. That is, they may stay in the U.S. for extended periods, working in various parts of the country, and return to Mexico for periodic visits.

Many of the commuters are U.S. citizens. They may compose as much as 25 percent of the group. For the most part they are Mexican-Americans who were born here, but for a variety of reasons prefer to live in Mexico and work in the U.S.

Since the Immigration and Naturalization Service does not keep records of commuters on a daily basis, it becomes very difficult to present more than estimates. The number of commuters varies according to the time of year, labor market fluctuations in the U.S., and economic fluctuations in Mexico.

On four occasions the Immigration and Naturalization Service has taken sample counts of the commuters, twice in 1963 (May 8 and 16), once in 1966 (January 11), and once in 1967

° For a history and definition of commuters, see Appendix I; 1c, 1d, 6, 7. See also North, 1970.

TABLE 1

COMMUTER WORKERS IDENTIFIED BY OCCUPATIONAL CLASS,
NOVEMBER 1 THROUGH DECEMBER 31, 1967 (DAILY AVERAGES)

Port	Industrial workers	Building trades and construction workers	Agricultural workers	Sales and service workers	Private household workers	Total
California:						
San Ysidro	2,005	409	2,827	1,950	344	7,535
Tecate	6	4	30	14	2	56
Calexico	195	93	6,810	517	75	7,690
Andrade	1	0	2	0	0	3
Arizona:						
San Luis	39	14	3,325	146	29	3,553
Lukeville	0	0	0	0	0	0
Sasabe	0	0	0	3	0	3
Nogales	179	136	6	682	115	1,118
Naco	3	31	10	47	3	94
Douglas	48	28	175	99	30	380
New Mexico:						
Columbus	2	1	26	1	0	30
Texas:						
El Paso:						
Sante Fe Bridge	1,801	844	1,088	2,725	1,388	7,846
Cordova	1,145	704	136	1,387	119	3,491
Ysleta	132	60	165	46	20	423
Fabens	60	14	195	1	9	279
Fort Hancock	3	1	46	0	3	53
Presidio	1	3	17	2	1	24
Del Rio	144	65	18	70	20	317
Eagle Pass	185	147	751	398	154	1,635
Laredo	106	212	321	1,825	205	2,669
Roma	1	7	54	10	1	73
Hidalgo	70	146	472	199	50	937
Progreso	0	6	41	2	1	50
Brownsville	724	215	298	632	148	1,917
	6,850	3,140	16,713*	10,756	2,717	40,176

SOURCE: Statement of Richard C. Haberstroh, District Director, United States Immigration and Naturalization Service. *The Impact of Commuter Aliens Along the Mexican and Canadian Borders.* Hearings before the Select Commission on Western Hemisphere Immigration. Part I, El Paso, Texas, January 26–27, 1968.
* Includes 7,743 agricultural workers who came to the border from the interior of the United States during the count and commenced working as commuters. It is anticipated these workers will return to the interior of the United States in the spring to work as migrants.

(November 1 to December 31). This latest count revealed the figures shown in Table 1. These figures are a sample for a given period of time. It is known that when counts are being taken many commuters, probably apprehensive about what is being planned or about their status, either do not cross into the U.S. or remain in the U.S. until the "danger" is over.

The controversy revolving around the commuting practice focuses on several issues: (1) the legal question, (2) the border economy, (3) the labor situation, and (4) the political aspects.

The Legal Question

The commuter is defined as an alien who has an immigrant visa, Form I-151 (green card), and who lives in Mexico and comes to the U.S. to work. The first step in attaining commuter status is to be admitted lawfully into the United States as an immigrant (Appendix I; 2). This is done by applying for an immigrant visa to a U.S. consular officer. An immigrant must meet all of the requirements of the Immigration and Nationality Act, he must obtain a labor certification showing that there is a shortage of workers in the U.S. in his particular occupation and that his entry will not have an adverse effect on the wages and working conditions of U.S. residents (Appendix I; 29, 33). If a commuter is unemployed for more than six months, except for uncontrollable circumstances such as illness or injury, he may lose his commuter status.

Although the commuting practice has been in existence for over forty years, an immigrant to the U.S., by law, should be a resident of the U.S. In the border situation, through custom, tradition, and interpretation of the law, the U.S. has created a "legal fiction" which equates "residence" with employment. This situation leads one to the conclusion that the immigration visa given to the commuter is nothing more than an alien work permit, the consequences of which, in many instances, are the exploitation of "cheap" labor.

The definition of the legal status of the commuter program has been avoided by the courts (*Amalgamated Meat Cutters* v. *Rogers*), thereby perpetuating this "legal fiction." Judge Philip Newman of Los Angeles has concluded, "from a legal point of view, the commuter program is contrary to law" (David North in WHI Hearings, Part I, 24).

Some 40,000 of these Mexican immigrant aliens are daily commuters. Unknown thousands are periodic "commuters," i.e., they may enter the U.S. for purposes of employment weekly, semimonthly, monthly or for longer periods.

Another group of "commuters" are those who hold Form I-186, a border-crossing permit. (See Appendix I; 40, 42.) This card has been issued for business, shopping, and pleasure. The card prohibits working in the U.S., and under the old regulations it was valid indefinitely. Since 1965 its validity has been restricted to four years, and it can be used for only seventy-two hours. Previously travel with the permit was not to exceed 150 miles from the border. Because of its abuse, however, new regulations were issued recently restricting the area of travel to twenty-five miles from the border, unless special permission is granted (Appendix I; 40).

It is estimated that in El Paso 2,500 to 3,000 of these cards are issued monthly and several hundred are canceled monthly, primarily for violation of the work restriction. It is further estimated that 75,000 citizens of Ciudad Juárez possess these cards (WHI Hearings, Part I, 1968; 9–11). In Brownsville 1,500 to 2,000 of these cards are issued monthly (WHI Hearings, Part III, 1968:12). According to John Killea, U.S. Consul General at Tijuana:

> Considerably in excess of 150,000 are estimated to be holding border-crossing cards issued by the Immigration and Naturalization Service at San Ysidro [California]. [WHI Hearings, Part II, 1968:16]

Los Angeles District Director George Rosenberg said:

> We picked up 16,000 illegal aliens this year. We have every reason to believe that most of them came in with those cards, although their practice is to divest themselves of the card before they are apprehended. Because they know there is going to be an apprehension made, it is a matter of when. So we can't tell from the alien when he came in with the card. They give us a lot of explanation as to how they came in which doesn't jibe with my experience. My experience is a large part of the illegal aliens we find in the United States made their entry with the I-186. If we know that or prove it later, the I-186 will be cancelled. [WHI Hearings, Part II, 1968:13]

How many aliens with a border-crossing card actually are daily commuters is unknown, but many, such as domestics, undoubtedly are.

Border Economy

The economic issue on the border with regard to commuters may be summarized in the following way. It is claimed that the economy of the two nations is interconnected and particularly so between the cities which face each other along the border. The concept of the twin city has developed on the border, suggesting the economic interdependence of the two cities. A rather large population exists in the Mexican twin city and the U.S. border city is generally dependent on the Mexican twin city for its economic existence, based on retail sales to Mexican nationals. Many of these Mexican nationals are dependent on the U.S. twin city for their employment. The U.S. provides many jobs for Mexican nationals, but on the other hand it is estimated that most of the money earned by Mexican nationals is spent in the United States.

Donald W. Holmberg of the El Paso Chamber of Commerce presents the following viewpoint:

> The Commission may question our concern for the welfare of the Mexican city of Juárez or why this estimated 50-million dollars in wages should not be earned by bona fide U.S. citizens. Aside from the fact that these people are our very good friends, the drawing of an arbitrary line through the middle of 750,000 people does not separate them culturally, socially, and, most of all, economically. And because it is estimated that about 85% of the wages earned by commuters in the El Paso area are spent in El Paso, we have a selfish interest. [WHI Hearings, Part I, 1968: 147]

It is generally true that the state of Texas pays among the lowest wages in the country. It is one of thirteen states which has no minimum wage. Twelve of these states are rural states, whereas Texas is a rich industrial state, producing 23 percent of the mineral wealth of the United States. It is also among the top three states in agricultural production and produces more from the sea than any other state in the Union. Yet one-third of its 10.7 million population live below the poverty level. (Senator Ralph Yarborough in WHI Hearings, Part I, 1968:188–190.)

Unemployment rates are typically higher in the border areas than they are in the state as a whole. According to a Department of Labor study:

> The Texas Employment Commission prepares and publishes unemployment estimates for 22 Texas cities. In 1966 these data revealed that unemployment in border towns was substantially greater than in interior cities. . . . High unemployment rates are indicative of labor surpluses, surpluses that in turn cause lower wage rates as employers find it unnecessary to bid up wages to attract workers. The fact that unemployment is heavy and wage rates are low in the border towns is not coincidental. Workers residing in Mexico contribute to the labor surplus by filling jobs that United States residents would otherwise have—and frequently take them at wage rates unacceptable to United States residents. [WHI Hearings, Part I, 1968:135]

Those favoring the commuter program are employers representing commercial and agricultural interests, the chambers of commerce of the various cities on both sides of the border, and of course the Mexican government. The arguments used range from the interconnected border economy, the international balance of payments, aid to developing nations, good-neighborliness, and custom and tradition, to threats that if changes do occur there might be retaliation on the part of Mexico, or that U.S. interests, both commercial and agricultural, might move to Mexico and operate from there.

Labor Issues

Since the commuters represent a large pool of unskilled labor they compete unfairly with American labor, primarily Mexican-Americans. Commuters then displace Mexican-American labor, a large part of whom join the agricultural migratory stream in search of jobs or better wages. Commuters depress the wage structure in the border area. Since opportunities for employment in Mexico are not abundant and the standard of living is not as high as in the U.S., commuters are willing to work for lower wages. It is also alleged that the commuter practice hampers, and in many instances prevents, the unionization of American labor. Many employers are also charged with the exploitation of labor and the use of commuters as strikebreakers (Appendix I; 39).

In arguing for some sort of control of the commuter situation, Henry Munoz, director of the Equal Opportunity Department of the Texas AFL-CIO, says: "They [commuters] are making it darned hard for us to bargain collectively for work and better wages. They are taking our right to bargain collectively with employers. . . . I would like to tell you the effect of the Green Card holder: Higher levels of unemployment, lower wages, difficulties in collective bargaining efforts, higher proportion of minimum wage violations along the Texas-Mexican border, and lousy working conditions, all because of the abundance of low-paid workers" (WHI Hearings, Part I, 1968:33).

U.S. labor organizations have been particularly vociferous in their complaints regarding the commuter practice. They have been especially concerned with the low wages paid, the unfair competition, the strikebreaking, and what they perceive as interference with unionization.

In a study prepared by the U.S. Department of Labor, in April, 1967, it is stated that wages for seasonal farm work in the Texas border area were over 30 percent less than in the rest of the state, that firms employing alien commuters tend to pay lower wages than those employing only U.S. residents, and that firms employing alien commuters frequently pay them less than what they pay U.S. residents for the same work. ". . . it is not just that the commuters settle for lower wages and a lower living standard. They also avoid much of the costs of public service in the United States, some of which they enjoy: Public highways, medical and police protection services, shopping facilities, and sometimes even schools. This further reduces the real income of U.S. residents" (WHI Hearings, Part I, 1968:125).

Growers sometimes argue that agriculture requires stoop labor which citizens of this country do not and will not perform. Yet thousands of these American citizens do in fact perform this type of labor throughout the United States.

The mayor of Brownsville, Texas, Honorable Antonio Gonzalez, says that in his estimation the problem of alien commuters has developed into a serious conflict between labor and the advocates of free enterprise who want to continue to conduct their businesses without interference by governmental agencies or labor unions. "It is my belief that a person who invests his or her money in some private endeavor should have the right to select employees of his choice for the operation of his business so long as such employees have a legal right to work in the United States. This belief, to my mind, is shared by most businessmen who are engaged in free enterprise" (WHI Hearings, Part III, 1968:140).

A housewife and clubwoman is concerned about a number of problems which might arise if the commuter status were changed. She says, "They [U.S. women] would have to leave their occupations if they were deprived of the household help they are now getting from over the border. There are simply not enough workers in the United States in the categories of laundress, nursemaid, housemaid, cook, and such to fill the need." If commuters were required to become residents of the United States, this same woman wonders whether they would then be allowed to bring their dependents. "This would make them all eligible for ADC and old age assistance for the children and the old aunts and grandmothers who now take care of the children while the mother is at work. This would prove to be an intolerable load to the already overloaded taxpayer" (WHI Hearings, Part III, 1968:136–137).

The testimony of Jerry Cohen, legal counsel for the United Farm Workers Organizing Committee, suggests that the green card problem is the most important problem hampering the organization of American workers. He states that it is the major stumbling block in the path of organized labor (WHI Hearings, Part II, 1968:113–114).

Any number of people made statements concerning the desirability of having Mexican commuters: city mayors, presidents of chambers of commerce, directors of international commerce, businessmen, importers and exporters, managers of radio stations, presidents of banks, presidents of international good-neighbor councils. Opposing statements were made by members of labor unions, persons representing U.S. workers, and many other U.S. citizens. Eight hundred and ten residents of Laredo, Texas, 486 residents of Laredo and Eagle Pass, Texas, and 1,257 residents of the lower Rio Grande valley together with representatives of Mexican-American organizations were moved to either petition or make statements against the commuter practice (WHI Hearings, Part III, 1968:152–153).

In a study supported by the Department of Labor, Dr. Brian Rungeling concludes that commuters depress wages only to the extent that they are part of a large pool of unskilled workers and occupy jobs that unemployed U.S. citizens are apparently willing and capable of holding (Rungeling, 1969:2).

Political Issues

William Hughes, American Consul General stationed in Juárez, Mexico, stated:

> I think the Commission would also be interested in the fact that this problem [commuters] was discussed fairly recently with the Foreign Minister of Mexico, Mr. Carrillo Flores, who indicated that in view of the fact that there were perhaps as many as 40,000, maybe even 50,000, commuters along the border whose total family members might equal as many as a quarter million people, that Mexico would certainly view adversely any action which the United States might take precipitately to change this long-held status by this number of people. But he at the same time indicated clearly that such matters are strictly the concern of the United States and that certainly Mexico could not and would not express any view on any proposed legislation dealing with the issuance of immigrant visas or dealing with the commuter problem. [WHI Hearings, Part I, 1968:13–14]

The political issues suggested by the practice of commuting are international in nature. It is claimed that it behooves the U.S. and Mexico to be good neighbors, a relationship which has been cherished by both nations and which would be upset if the commuter practice were tampered with.

If legislation were enacted to restrict the program, it is further claimed that one could expect reprisals from Mexico, particularly of an economic nature. These could include regulations prohibiting Mexicans from buying in the U.S. and restricting imports from the U.S. In the opinion of Don M. Irwin, of the Border Cities Association:

> If this legislation were passed [S. 2790, placing certain restrictions on commuters] it would bring immediate and effective reprisals from Mexico, who would diligently enforce their laws. [WHI Hearings, Part I, 1968:151]

David T. Lopez, a field representative for the AFL-CIO in Texas testified:

The final note of absurdity in The Chamber of Commerce argument is that the dire threat it holds already is here. About five weeks ago, the Mexican government announced it was deploying numerous special customs agents along the border to curtail by 80%, and eventually eliminate, the importation of retail goods from the United States. I feel confident that no sleep was lost by the Mexican government officials over whether the United States would retaliate by banning commuters.

The interest of the Chamber of Commerce and other business and employer groups is simply to maintain low wages and discourage the formation of unions. [WHI Hearings, Part I, 1968: 233]

The other argument for maintaining the commuter practice is that it has existed for some forty-seven years through custom, tradition, and interpretation of the law, and thus commuters have long established "rights" which should not be revoked.

General Social Issues

The immigrant visa clearly indicates that the immigrant is to reside in a country for which the visa is issued. In the case of Mexican and Canadian "immigrants" who falsely declare that their place of residence will be in the U.S. and who plan only to work in the U.S. and live in their native country, it would appear that the law is being subverted. The courts, however, have not been clear in their interpretations.

Whenever attempts are made at either clarification or change in this special (and perhaps illegal) commuter status the various interests in the U.S. choose sides, as we have discussed above. Besides the legal, economic, labor, and political arguments, social issues may be brought into the question. The chambers of commerce, businesses and other employers, and most governmental officials generally take the position that if the residence requirements were enforced, great hardships would ensue.

It is alleged that if a commuter immigrant had to live in the U.S. there would be a considerable break-up of the family structure, the reasoning being that commuters do not really want to live in the U.S. Thus only the commuter would seek residence here, leaving his family in Mexico. (Curiously enough, those who use this argument are, in general, the same people who supported the Bracero Program, which in fact necessitated extremely long absences from home for the bracero laborer.)

On the other hand, the argument goes, if the commuter were to decide, as he could, to bring his family with him to the U.S., then the border cities would be inundated by the movement of several hundred thousand persons seeking housing. Should this occur, other problems would follow, namely, greatly increased demands upon facilities and services. Schools, teachers, hospitals, public utilities, parks and recreational facilities, police and fire departments, and welfare services could find themselves overwhelmed by the influx of people. Organized labor and others argue that such a situation, under present wage structures, would present severe problems to cities, but with "decent" wages, problems would not be so great.

As indicated earlier, the border area has long been a magnet in northern Mexico, extending its drawing power to the capital and beyond.

Over the years the American invasion into Mexico (and Latin America) has been phenomenal and in large proportions. There is hardly a product produced in the United States that is unknown in Mexico and the usual commodities (soft drinks, toiletries, notions, dry goods, steel and paper products) abound. The capital invested in the development of industry and commerce, with its subsequent advertising and other promotion, has whetted appetites for the "good life." And where, but at the source, is the "good life" more readily attainable for those on the fringes of society? The presence and influence of the United States in Mexico is established beyond a doubt. The fact that U.S. tourism is Mexico's number-one industry attests to this. Crossings of persons from the United States into Mexico numbered 59,773,793 in the year ending June 30, 1968. For whatever reason and in whatever way, the gringo and things gringo are well known in Mexico.

But there are also many Mexicans (or Mexican-Americans) and things Mexican in the United States. Although the Spanish-speaking population is concentrated in the Southwest, this particular influence extends to greater or lesser degrees throughout the country. Noticeable concentrations occur in such centers as Chicago and Chicago Heights in Illinois; Hammond, East Chicago, and Gary in Indiana; Detroit, Flint, Saginaw, and

Lansing in Michigan; Cleveland and Toledo in Ohio, and Kansas City in Kansas. There is not a single state in the Union which does not have Mexicans (legal or illegal) or Mexican-Americans.

The biggest drawing card for Mexicans has been employment opportunities in this country, coupled with great unemployment in Mexico. This is not so much because of a need for a great industrial labor pool, but because of agricultural employment and low-status service occupations (waitresses, bell boys, custodians, clerical workers, and domestics) which generally pay low wages (by U.S. standards) and for this reason are not very attractive to U.S. citizens.

This study suggests that the "open border" has existed from approximately 1849, when the boundary was created, until 1930. After the repatriation of Mexicans following the Great Depression in the U.S., conditions dictated a tightening-up of border population movements. World War II, however, created a demand for foreign labor which was met by contractual agreements between Mexico and the U.S. This demand for cheap labor gave further impetus to the internal population movements from central Mexico to the border region.

In historical terms both Mexicans and Americans have moved freely across the border, Americans in search of entertainment, tourist attractions, and investment possibilities. Mexicans have moved north in search of goods, some tourism, but mainly for employment.

ii: *The Illegal Mexican Alien**

The wetback is a hungry human being. His need of food and clothing is immediate and pressing. He is a fugitive and it is as a fugitive that he lives. Under the constant threat of apprehension and deportation, he cannot protest or appeal, no matter how unjustly he is treated. Law operates against him but not for him. Those who capitalize on the legal disability of the wetbacks are numerous and their devices are many and various. [President's Commission, 1951:78]

Our main contention concerning the illegal Mexican aliens is that their presence in the U.S is directly related to the interests of employers in securing an ample supply of cheap labor. In order to explain the origin and cyclical influx of illegal Mexican aliens attention must focus on the desire and recruitment practices of agribusiness with regard to Mexican labor. We find, for example, that agribusiness has been influential in the outcome of state and federal legislation, which means that its influence has affected immigration policy. It is in such a manner that immigration restrictions have been periodically relaxed and special migration treaties enacted. The relaxation of immigration restrictions permitting the entrance of Mexican labor during World War I and the Bracero Program, initiated during World War II, are two outstanding examples. U.S. immigration policies, through their selective application and periodic relaxation along the Mexican border merely regulated if they did not insure the realization of the interests of agribusiness.

* This chapter was originally written by Gilbert Cardenas.

We will begin with a brief review of the movement of aliens over the U.S.-Mexican border, focusing primarily on the selective enforcement of U.S. immigration laws. Then we will attempt to specify the relationship between the process of labor recruitment and the process of Mexican immigration, indicating the sociological basis of what is popularly referred to in the literature as an "open border" as well as the conditions that lead to a "closed border." Then our discussion will center in on the relationship between the Bracero Program and the influx of illegal aliens.

In the final section, we will discuss the role of the Border Patrol in the transition from a relatively open border to a relatively closed border.

Illegal Aliens and Immigration Laws

The following factors are related to the early situation along the U.S.-Mexican border: (1) the application of the Chinese Exclusion Laws and the gentleman's agreement, (2) the 1921 and 1924 Quota Laws as they were applied along the U.S.-Mexican border, and (3) the selective enforcement practices of the U.S. Border Patrol.

As early as 1903, the Commissioner of Immigration recognized the need for guarding the United States-Mexican border. Nevertheless, the initial concern was to prevent the entry of Chinese aliens. As a result of the Chinese Exclusion Law passed in 1882, the primary border problem became the issue of the smuggling of Chinese rather than the entry of Mexicans. In the eyes of immigration authorities, the Chinese were the first "wetbacks," and it was in the interest of excluding Chinese that the first efforts were made to establish a border guard.

> Aliens of the inadmissable classes now find it quite as difficult to gain access to this country through Canada, which was formerly an open door to them, as at a seaport of the United States. As one of the results it may be reasonably anticipated that the next means to be resorted to by such aliens will be the Mexican boundary—a point of weakness in our defense from undesirable immigration that has already been discovered and utilized by the most resourceful of alien peoples—the Chinese. To strengthen this line will be one of the immediate necessities, involving the assignment of active, young, and intelligent officers, under a capable and

experienced general control, to guard the long stretch from the Pacific Coast to the Gulf of Mexico. [U.S. Bureau of Immigration, 1903:63]

During this period from 1903 to 1921, the Chinese and other Oriental groups continued to receive maximum attention from the border guard. Mexican immigration and border crossings during this same period did not preoccupy the attention of immigration authorities. The U.S. Army, however, was quite active in its attempts to capture Mexican raiders and Villistas. These actions culminated in the Punitive Expedition of 1916 led by General Pershing (Clendenen, 1969). This invasion of Mexico was a direct violation of Mexico's sovereignty, as was the earlier 1914 invasion at Vera Cruz. In this period, immigration authorities reportedly lacked an adequate force to guard the Mexican border and, perhaps, were unwilling to apply the law to Mexicans because of the so-called spirit of cooperation established by the local residents and immigration authorities. It is doubtful if the head tax of 1882, the Contract Labor Law of 1885, or the literacy test of 1917 initially restricted Mexican immigration and border crossings. At best, these restrictions merely stimulated *illegal* immigration (U.S. Department of Labor, Annual Report of Commissioner-General of Immigration, 1923:16). At any rate, the volume and proportion of Mexican immigration in this period was relatively insignificant when compared to the influx of European aliens and the immigration problems of the East Coast. (See Table 2.)

With the passage of the Quota Act of 1921, smuggling of European aliens across the Mexican border into the United States increased. "The problem of stopping the inflow of European aliens subject to the quota law had almost entirely displaced the Chinese smuggling with which the border service had to contend for so many years" (U.S. Department of Labor, Annual Report of Commissioner-General of Immigration, 1923:26). In 1923 the Commissioner-General reported that an increase of aliens from Europe and the Near East rather than from China necessitated the "revival" or creation of a border guard or patrol to perform strictly police work in the prevention of alien border running. In the same report the Commissioner-General stated that "the peoples of Canada and Mexico wholesomely respect our immigration laws; it

TABLE 2

NUMBER OF MEXICAN IMMIGRANTS COMPARED WITH ALL
IMMIGRANTS, FIVE-YEAR PERIODS, 1900–1964

Period[a]	Mexican[b]	Total	Mexican as % of Total
1900–1904	2,259	3,255,149	.07
1905–1909	21,732	4,947,239	.44
1910–1914	82,588	5,174,701	1.60
1915–1919	91,075	1,172,679	7.77
1920–1924	249,248	2,774,600	8.98
1925–1929	238,527	1,520,910	15.68
1930–1934	19,200	426,953	4.50
1935–1939	8,737	272,422	3.21
1940–1944	16,548	203,589	8.13
1945–1949	37,742	653,019	5.78
1950–1954	78,723	1,099,035	7.16
1955–1959	214,746	1,400,233	15.34
1960–1964	217,827	1,419,013	15.35

SOURCE: Annual Reports of the U.S. Immigration and Naturalization Service and its predecessor agencies. (Grebler, 1966:8)
[a] Fiscal Years.
[b] Classified by country of birth, except for the periods 1935–1939 and 1940–1944 in which the data refer to Mexico as the country of last permanent residence. This classification had to be adopted because the reports for several years in these periods do not furnish data by country of birth. The statistics for periods for which both classifications are reported indicate that numerical differences are relatively small. The "country of birth" classification was adopted here as the basic one not only because it is definitionally superior but also because detailed characteristics of immigrants are reported on this basis.

may be reasonably expected that this will continue unless it so happens that a limit is put upon the numbers who may come from those countries" (U.S. Department of Labor, Annual Report of Commissioner-General of Immigration, 1923:26).

Through the years an effective apparatus had been developed to guard the border. The El Paso district supervisor's description of the four-line defense strategy in 1923 illustrates the structure of the Border Patrol apparatus:

When Chinese smuggling was rampant on this border, a force at least approximating that required to cope with the situation was available. There were river guards to apprehend, if possible, the aliens and smugglers in the act of illegal entry; mounted men to pursue if the aliens eluded the vigilance of the officers at the points of crossing and proceeded overland by wagon or automobile; men to open and inspect freight cars before they left the border towns, and men to inspect all passenger trains leaving such towns. All these constituted the first line of defense. The second line of defense consisted of inspectors at strategical interior points on all railroads running north from the border, when another opening of freight cars and a thorough inspection of both passenger and freight trains occurred. The officers at these points, likewise, covered the highways for Chinese travelling afoot, by wagon, or in automobiles. . . . It was found that smugglers accompanying aliens from the border unloaded them from trains—both passenger and freight—and detoured them around the inspection points. Third and even fourth lines of defense were therefore established on some of the railroads at points farther removed from the border. [U.S. Department of Labor, Annual Report of Commissioner-General of Immigration, 1923:18–19]

As early as 1924, the Commissioner-General of Immigration reported that the border could be secured despite a limited number of border officers:

For a number of years the Immigration Service has maintained a small and widely scattered force of mounted guards on the Mexican border for the purpose of preventing alien smuggling. Ordinarily this force numbered somewhat less than 60 men, most of whom were especially chosen because of their knowledge of border conditions, and they have rendered conspicuous service in enforcing the law in that difficult territory. In fact, this small force has accomplished so much in the way of apprehending smugglers and aliens that in some sections of that vast southwest territory border running has come to be regarded as an extremely hazardous occupation. [U.S. Department of Labor, Annual Report of Commissioner-General of Immigration, 1924:23]

But even in January 1924 the question of Mexican immigration did not concern the Immigration Commissioner as did the immigration of other alien groups crossing the Mexican border. Subsequently the number of European immigrants decreased, while the number and proportion of Mexicans to the total volume of immigrants increased. By the time Mexican immigration (legal and illegal) became a major problem, the Border Patrol had been given official legislative recognition, for in 1924 Congress appropriated approximately one million dollars for the purpose of extending the land border patrol (U.S. Department of Labor, Annual Report of Commissioner-General of Immigration, 1924:23).

1915–1930

The selective enforcement of U.S. immigration laws along the U.S.-Mexican border, together with the recruiting practices of U.S. employers, i.e., advertising and contracting in Mexico, and advertising and contracting in the Southwest, actually induced the northward migration of Mexican campesinos and, for all practical purposes, legitimatized their entry into the U.S. (Montavon, 1930:272). Unable and in many cases unwilling to find other sources of labor, U.S. employers, particularly in the agricultural and railroad industries, looked toward Mexico.

During World War I, at the request of U.S. industrialists, the provisions of the recently enacted immigration laws relating to the head tax, contract labor laws, and literacy requirements were waived for Mexican laborers by the Commissioner-General of Immigration with the approval of the Secretary of Labor and under the authority of Section 3 of the Ninth Proviso of the Immigration Act of 1917.

From 1917 to 1921, more than 72,862 Mexican aliens were legally admitted under this special departmental order. According to one report, by 1929 34,922 of the aliens had returned to Mexico, 414 were reported dead, 494 had been given permanent residence, another 21,400 had deserted or disappeared, and the remaining 15,632 were still with their original employers (Morrison, 1929:9).

From the standpoint of the receiving society (United States), the departmental order of 1918 represented the first widespread dependency on such labor in the Southwest. From the standpoint of the sending country (Mexico), the departmental order represented the first time in U.S. immigration policy that Mexicans were made an exception to the general rule. In effect, employment opportunities in selected industries in the Southwest were extended to Mexican nationals, stimulating the already appreciable northward migration of the Mexican campesino.

Although the departmental order was initiated as a war-time measure, it was not terminated until long after the war ended. Nevertheless, the desire and recruitment practices of employers for laborers did not terminate but, in fact, were extended and intensified.

Wanting a large pool of cheap labor to expand their industries, Southwestern industrialists continued to encourage the movement of Mexicans across the border. Because of the revolutionary conditions in Mexico, it was relatively easy for enterprising United States industrialists to take advantage of the poor condition of the Mexican campesino. Largely because of the wage differential existing between employment in the United States and employment in Mexico, the Mexican campesino was easily induced northward. In the Southwest the campesino became locked in a similar system of peonage yet under different conditions of management.

Competition for Mexican labor among employers in the Southwest arose because of the labor demands of their industries, particularly as they affected agriculture. Not satisfied with the mere assurance of a sufficient supply, the industrialists sought and eventually attained an abundant supply of labor, one large enough to enable them to expand their industries as markets expanded. The relative ability of labor to benefit from the increased production and expansion was undermined at the same time. It was in this context that southwestern industrialists sought Mexican labor.

Industrialists from the Northwest and Midwest induced Mexicans to their own sections in the same way. The net effect of the northward migration of domestic farm workers, i.e., Mexican-Americans and resident Mexican aliens, was a reduction of the size of the labor pool available to the southwestern industrialists. Unwilling to compete and unable to legally stop the recruiting and contracting practices of the northwestern and midwestern industrialists, the southwestern industrialists again reasoned that more Mexican nationals were needed. In the long run, the recruitment process served to create a large labor pool on both sides of the border.

The main point that must be emphasized is that this process of procuring Mexican labor became the basic and most significant feature underlying most Mexican migration to the United States as well as determining the very nature and condition of the domestic Mexican migrant.

Considering the economic situation of the Mexican campesino, the time spent in being legally processed at the border, the low risk of being apprehended and deported by the Border Patrol because of that service's selective enforcement practices, and, most importantly, the assurance of being employed in the U.S., large numbers of Mexican campesinos continued to enter the U.S. illegally. Even when the laws were being enforced, it was done in a manner that nearly insured the illegal status of the Mexican campesino. Many Mexicans from the interior of Mexico came to the border, as the news spread of the relative ease of entering the U.S. to work, but found that the laws were being enforced.* Being far from home and still reasonably assured employment in the U.S., the campesino had but one realistic alternative, to cross the border and enter the United States illegally.

Taking issue with the census figures showing that over 500,000 Mexicans illegally entered the U.S. between 1920 to 1930, the Commissioner-General of Immigration claimed that only 289,000 illegal aliens were located for that same period (U.S. Department of Labor, Annual Report of the Secretary of Labor, 1935:78).

The 1930's

Among the factors operating to restrict Mexican immigration into the United States and to encourage large-scale emigration in the 1930's were: (1) the Deportation Act of March 4, 1929, (2) the May 4, 1929 law, and (3) the Great Depression. While the act of March 4, 1929, rendered aliens liable to deportation on various counts, the May 4, 1929 law made it a felony for a deported alien to reenter the U.S. illegally. Equipped with these two laws, along with the existing immi-

---

* Under the provisions the 1924 Quota Law, despite the fact that Mexico and other Western Hemisphere countries were not brought under quota, all immigrants including Mexican were required to pay a $10 consular fee. This $10 visa fee together with the $8 head tax, the $2 medical examination fee, the literacy test, and the contract labor laws, when applied vigorously, could substantially reduce the number of legal Mexican entries and, by extension, increase the number of illegal entries. For example, in 1924, 87,648 legal Mexican immigrants reportedly entered the United States. In 1925 the number of legal Mexican immigrants was reduced to 32,378, largely because of a temporary, but effective, interest in applying the immigration laws along the border.

gration laws, no additional legislation was needed to counter-act Mexican immigration, only the application and enforcement of the law.

Commenting on the creation of an atmosphere of fear among Mexicans already in the United States, Robert McLean wrote:

> It may be indefinite, but it is very real; and the quality is standard all the way from California to Texas. . . . and that *fear* hovers over every Mexican colony in the Southwest is a fact that all who come in contact with them can readily attest. They fear examination by the Border Patrol when they travel; they fear arrest; they fear jail; they fear deportation; and whereas they used to write inviting friends, they now urge them not to come. [McLean, 1930:29]

Corresponding to the adverse effects caused by the Great Depression was a renewed interest in preventing the entry of illegal Mexican aliens and greater efforts to deport deportable Mexican aliens. And, of course, deportable Mexican aliens were among those who were permitted to work the fields during prosperity, yet who found themselves displaced along with other Mexican farm workers, because of the widespread unemployment of U.S. citizens.

The "back-to-the-land" movement (Thompson, 1937:22) was so great at this time that during the early period of the Depression (1930–1933) the number of persons arriving at farms from cities, towns, and villages tended to approximate the number of persons leaving farms for cities, towns, and villages. (See Table 3.) So great were adverse effects of the Depression upon the Mexican farm worker that in 1935 Mexican emigration exceeded immigration by more than five to one. Only 1,232 Mexicans were admitted for permanent residence, whereas 6,629 returned to Mexico (U.S. Department of Labor, Annual Report of the Secretary of Labor, 1935:85).

Concluding this section on the illegal Mexican alien, we have seen how a relatively open border was transformed to a relatively closed one. The border was opened to Mexican labor with the departmental order during World War I and was closed with the advent of the Great Depression. During the Depression "wetback" labor was displaced, illegal Mexican aliens were deported, and Mexican entrants were either

TABLE 3

MOVEMENT OF PERSONS TO AND FROM FARMS:
UNITED STATES, 1920–1925

Year	Persons Arriving at Farms from Cities, Towns, and Villages	Persons Leaving Farms for Cities, Towns, and Villages	Net Movement from Cities, Towns, and Villages to Farms	Net Movement from Farms to Cities, Towns, and Villages
1920	560,000	896,000	. . . . .	336,000
1921	759,000	1,323,000	. . . . .	564,000
1922	1,115,000	2,252,000	. . . . .	1,137,000
1923	1,355,000	2,162,000	. . . . .	807,000
1924	1,581,000	2,068,000	. . . . .	487,000
1925	1,336,000	2,038,000	. . . . .	702,000
1926	1,427,000	2,334,000	. . . . .	907,000
1927	1,705,000	2,162,000	. . . . .	457,000
1928	1,698,000	2,120,000	. . . . .	422,000
1929	1,604,000	2,081,000	. . . . .	477,000
1930	1,611,000	1,823,000	. . . . .	212,000
1931	1,546,000	1,566,000	. . . . .	20,000
1932	1,777,000	1,511,000	266,000	. . . . .
1933	944,000	1,225,000	. . . . .	281,000
1934	700,000	1,051,000	. . . . .	351,000
1935	825,000	1,211,000	. . . . .	386,000
1920–1924	5,370,000	8,701,000	. . . . .	3,331,000
1925–1929	7,770,000	10,735,000	. . . . .	2,965,000
1930–1934	6,578,000	7,176,000	. . . . .	598,000

SOURCE: United States Department of Agriculture, Bureau of Agricultural Economics, Farm Population Estimates, January 1, 1936. Released October 27, 1936. (Births and deaths not taken into account.) (Thompson, 1937:19)

prevented at the border from illegally entering the U.S. or discouraged from coming to the border. Again we turn to McLean to illustrate our point:

> Nonetheless, there are certain elements of injustice in the new border policy. For ten years, the Mexican peon had surely been the Atlas holding upon his broad shoulders the economic life of the Southwest. He has bent his back over every field, toiled on every mile of railroad, and poured his sweat into every cubic yard of concrete. We have needed him; we have felt that we could not get along without him. And when our need was most acute in the industrial epoch which followed the war, we forgot our own immigration laws. Now that the acute need has passed away, by a stricter interpretation we are uprooting these people and sending them home. By actual deportations, or by "putting the fear of God" into their hearts, we are thrusting them into an economic order with which they have grown unfamiliar. Most of them have been conscious of doing no wrong. And when they steal back across the line to reestablish themselves in the social and economic order to which we have accustomed them, they are thrown in jail as common felons. The injustice comes not from any particular border policy, but rather because we have had no consistent policy. [McLean, 1930:55]

Braceros and Illegal Mexican Aliens

With the renewed prosperity caused by World War II, we find a renewed interest in acquiring cheap labor by regional agriculturalists and a corresponding interest on the part of the Mexican campesino in finding work in the United States.

Since 1940, the number of illegal Mexican aliens has exceeded the number entering legally. (See Burma, 1954:44.) According to labor economist Adolf Sturmthal, the Mexican government put the need of economic development ahead of financial stability and fostered capital formation through inflationary policies which increase the rate of profits while decreasing labor's share of the national income (Hancock, 1959:30). Real wages were stable or declining in many industries and in nearly all phases of agriculture in Mexico (Hancock, 1959:30). Assuming, then, that in the period from 1930 to 1940 the relative status of the Mexican peasant was not significantly bettered and that his socio-economic status may be held constant since 1940, the migration potential of the

Mexican campesino during the 1940's was not significantly greater than his migration potential throughout the 1930's. Thus to explain the phenomenal increase of illegal Mexican aliens located in the United States during the 1940's, greater attention must be given to changes occuring in the United States than to those occurring in Mexico.

Vested interests in cheap labor attracted and even lured the Mexican campesino to the United States. Such interests sought to exploit the wage differential between earnings in Mexico and those possible in the U.S. But wage differences are never in themselves sufficient for insuring migration, at least not on the Mexican border. The migration of Mexican workers to the United States, then, is directly related to the desire of U.S. agriculturalists and industrialists to attract Mexican laborers.

The creation and maintenance of the Bracero Program arose out of the interests of growers and their influence on public policy. As it worked out, the Bracero Program actually stimulated unlawful migration into the United States. During the Bracero Program, the size of the Mexican migration (legal and illegal) was governed by the U.S.'s ability to absorb workers rather than by a limitation of the supply of Mexican workers (Hancock, 1959:29). As early as 1942 Mexican campesinos began migrating north with the intention of working in the United States. The northward movement, however, was encouraged by advertising by American farmers and increased as the news of available work spread in the months that followed (Scruggs, 1961:151).

Other scholars have supported the thesis that the Bracero Program actually stimulated illegal Mexican migration into the United States. According to Eleanor Hadley the only explanation for this increased illegal migration in the period 1944–1954 was the initiation of the Mexican contract labor program.

Apparently, the relation between this Mexican contract labor program and the spiraling illegal immigration was this: Contract workers returned with exciting tales of the money that could be earned in the United States. The next year these same workers wanted to repeat their performance and their neighbors wanted to join. The result was that there were many more Mexicans who wanted to come to the United States than there were certifications of need issued by the Secretary of Labor. Further, managing to be among the workers selected by the Mexican officials for the program characteristically required the persuasion of a bribe. Thus it seemed to many much simpler to seek American employment on their own. [Hadley, 1956:344]

Leo Grebler also pointed out the parallelism between the Bracero Program and the influx of illegal Mexican aliens:

> Illegal migration of "wetbacks," however, continued even after the initiation of the bracero program. By going this route, Mexican laborers could save the time, inconvenience, and expenses involved in travelling to their government's recruitment centers (of which there seem to have been too few), as well as the official fees and the unofficial commissions which appear to have been exacted by middlemen. And American farm enterprises continued to offer employment to all comers. The growers could avoid the red tape of the bracero program, save the $25 bond required for each worker and the $15 contracting fee imposed by the United States government, and circumvent the minimum employment period and the wage and other safeguards built into the official arrangements. Thus, Mexican braceros and wetbacks often worked side by side on ranches and farms. . . . [Grebler, 1966:32]

The hiring of illegal Mexican aliens increased as employers, dissatisfied with the Bracero Program, sought to maximize their profits. Texas farmers, because of Mexico's refusal to extend the Bracero Program into their state, probably hired more illegal Mexican aliens than any other state. We have reason to believe also that even those farmers who were not immediately interested in hiring illegal Mexican aliens were forced to do so in order to compete with other growers who used such labor in their fields. (See President's Commission, 1951:83.)

By 1944, the magnitude of this illegal border traffic reached new levels. The entire period from 1944 to 1954 may well become known as the "wetback" decade of American immigration history (Hadley, 1956:334). The number of aliens expelled mounted each year, from 26,689 in 1944 to 1,075,168 in 1954. (See Table 4.) Meanwhile, neither Mexico nor the United States was willing to accept responsibility for the phenomenal increase. Scruggs's account of this situation is particularly illuminating:

The two countries were not even remotely agreed on a solution to the problem. Owing partly to a genuine belief that the problem was more an American than a Mexican concern, and partly to opposition to the added cost of augmenting its border force and its disinclination to place further controls on its citizens, Mexico was unwilling to increase its efforts to keep the workers home and suggested that the remedy lay in American action against employers of wetbacks. The United States, wishing to dodge the sensitive issue of penalties and believing that Mexico was not carrying its share of the burden of enforcement, increased somewhat its vigilance along the border and demanded that Mexico do likewise. [Scruggs, 1961:158]

TABLE 4

MEXICAN ILLEGAL ALIENS REPORTED

Year	Total	Year	Total	Year	Total
1924	4,614	1939	9,376	1954	1,075,168
1925	2,961	1940	8,051	1955	242,608
1926	4,047	1941	6,082	1956	72,442
1927	4,495	1942	DNA	1957	44,451
1928	5,529	1943	8,189	1958	37,242
1929	8,538	1944	26,689	1959	30,196
1930	18,319	1945	63,602	1960	29,651
1931	8,409	1946	91,456	1961	29,817
1932	7,116	1947	182,986	1962	30,272
1933	15,875	1948	179,385	1963	39,124
1934	8,910	1949	278,538	1964	43,844
1935	9,139	1950	458,215	1965	55,349
1936	9,534	1951	500,000	1966	89,751
1937	9,535	1952	543,538	1967	108,327
1938	8,684	1953	865,318	1968	151,705
				1969	201,636
Total					5,627,371

SOURCES: 1924–1941: Annual Report of the Secretary of Labor; 1942–1960: Special compilation of the Immigration and Naturalization Service reported to us; 1961–1969: Annual Report, I. & N. Service.

NOTE: The Immigration and Naturalization Service was in the Department of Labor until 1941. Since then it has been in the Department of Justice. Over the years a variety of categories have been used to report Mexican illegal aliens, with some inconsistency. This table reflects these inconsistencies. *Aliens deported* is a category that is consistently used for reporting Mexican illegal aliens but does not include all Mexican illegal aliens apprehended. It refers to those aliens forcefully expelled from the U.S. under warrant procedures. Mention is made of illegal entrants who are not allowed to remain in the U.S. These are reported as departing

Legalizing Illegals

A sizeable portion of the efforts to control the illegal traffic, however, occurred in a highly questionable manner. As a result of discussions held between Mexico and the United States in 1947, it was agreed that the United States give the subject of illegal entrants further study and that illegal aliens still in the United States be legalized by contracting them at the border as braceros to assure them decent treatment (Scruggs, 1951:158). Prior to this agreement, contracting was primarily the responsibility of the governments and the recruitment of Mexican laborers was done in Mexico City. Under the new practice, Mexican illegal aliens were returned to Mexico temporarily if only momentarily (as they put one foot across the boundary) and subsequently "recruited" under contract with employers in the United States. Commenting on this situation, Rasmussen wrote, "the return of illegal migrants to Mexico and their subsequent recruitment under contract with employers in the United States . . . appeared to be an opening for making direct employer-worker agreements with Mexicans who had not been in the United States" (Rasmussen, 1951:220).

The interim agreement of 1949 continued the practice of "wringing out wetbacks" begun in 1947.

Article 3 of that agreement provided that "Mexican agricultural workers who, on the effective date of this agreement, are

---

without the benefit of deportation warrant procedures after showing their willingness to depart. The following categories have also been used: *Aliens debarred* from entry (Annual Report of the Commissioner-General of Immigration, 1924: 12–13; 125–129); *Voluntary removals* (Annual Report of the Secretary of Labor, 1931:53–55); *Voluntary departures* (Annual Report of the Secretary of Labor, 1932:73); *Forced departures* without deportation warrant (Annual Report of the Secretary of Labor, 1939:97; 1940:110); *Required departures* (Annual Report of the Secretary of Labor, 1940:110). No data were available for 1942. The figures for 1943–1960 were furnished by the I. & N. Service under *Mexican Illegal Aliens Apprehended* (this includes deportations and voluntary departures). The figures for 1961–1969 are taken from the Annual Reports of those years under the category *Deportable Aliens Found and/or Located*. Even within the same report there are inconsistencies. In 1963, for example, on the same page, two figures are presented for *Deportable Mexican Aliens;* one is 38,866, the other 39,124 (Annual Report of Immigration and Naturalization Service, 1964:8).

illegally in the United States may be employed only under a contract approved pursuant to this agreement, and their immigration status will be adjusted accordingly. Such illegal workers when they are located in the United States shall be given preference for employment under outstanding United States Employment Service certifications." [Galarza, 1964:63]

According to Galarza's account of the politics of the "wetback decade," Public Law 78 was amended to authorize this "storm-and-drag method" of obtaining labor by drying out wetbacks (Galarza, 1964:69).

The process of "legalizing illegals" was widespread enough for the President's Commission on Migratory Labor to characterize it as "the dominant feature of the Mexican farm-labor program not only for 1947, but also for the years since" (President's Commission, 1951:38). According to their report a total of 74,600 Mexican nationals were brought under contract from the interior of Mexico from 1947 to 1949, and 142,000 illegal Mexican aliens already in the United States were put under contract and allowed to return to work, having thus been subjected to the magic of legalization (President's Commission, 1951:53).

The Border Patrol

It appears to us, as Saunders and Leonard (1951:14) reported, that the official group with whom the illegal Mexican alien has the most numerous contacts is the U.S. Immigration and Naturalization Service, particularly the officers of the Border Patrol. When considering the proposition that in the determination of U.S. Immigration policy Mexicans have been welcomed as laborers rather than citizens, it appears that the U.S. Immigration Service and its subdivision has been the most instrumental agent in effecting this policy.

Although one of the chief functions of the Border Patrol was to apprehend and exclude illegal aliens, it seems that in practice the Border Patrol functioned primarily to regulate the numbers that were already in the country.

Other writers, observing the situation of the illegal Mexican alien, have reported the regulatory function of the Border Patrol. As Saunders so clearly described it, "to allow enough in to permit the work to be done rapidly and cheaply, which, of course, means a surplus, and yet keep the number below the point at which wetbacks would overrun the Valley" (Saunders, 1951:15).

> The border could be effectively closed to wetbacks—nearly all Inspectors agree to that. But it cannot be closed without strong support and backing of their efforts on either the state or national level and at least a minimum of co-operation from local people. The role of the Border Patrol at present is like that of a balance wheel. They let in enough wetbacks to do the local work quickly and cheaply; but they send out enough to prevent serious over-crowding. One Inspector laughingly tells of the reaction of a local farmer to his suggestion that the Border Patrol retire a hundred miles north and allow wetbacks free access to the Valley. "Don't do that," the farmer said. "In a week they'd be overrunning the place, camping on our lawns, swarming everywhere. And there wouldn't be enough local police to handle them. What we want of the Border Patrol is to let in enough wetbacks for us to get our crops harvested and to keep the others out." . . . And that is about what they get. [Saunders and Leonard, 1951:82]

An American journalist wrote:

> Border Patrol officers worked around the clock to get the workers away from the border into the fields. Then, the needs supplied, the bars went up again and the officers returned to rounding up the illegal entries found in the El Paso Valley. [Leibson, 1949:15]

George Sanchez, long familiar with the border situation, gave a similar account of the role of the Border Patrol:

> The most dismaying aspect of this unsavory picture is the fact that govermental agencies, notably the Immigration Service and Employment Service, are participating in the introduction and employment of these thousands of wetbacks. [Sanchez, 1949:28]

More important, however, is the context in which the process of regulation occurs. It appears that the transition from a relatively open border to a relatively closed border occurs in *cycles* depending on the demands of the U.S. economy, particularly as such demands affect the Southwest. The relaxation of immigration policy, the relaxation of enforcement, and the employment of illegal Mexican aliens appear related to these cycles. The movement of Mexicans over the border appears to be related to the efforts of U.S. employers to encourage the relaxation of immigration restriction and enforcement at boom times or in extended periods of prosperity, whereas, the greatest efforts to clear out Mexicans occurs in the anticipation of a recession or during times of widespread unemployment.

It is in this manner that a seemingly unconcerned society becomes concerned:

> When the work is done, neither the farmer nor the community wants the wetback around. The number of apprehensions and deportations tends to rise very rapidly at the close of a seasonal work period. This can be interpreted not alone to mean that the immigration officer suddenly goes about his work with renewed zeal and vigor, but rather that at this time of the year "cooperation" in law enforcement by farm employers and townspeople rapidly undergoes considerable improvement. [President's Commission, 1951:78]

At this point it is necessary to distinguish between the "routine" and periodic operations of the Border Patrol and a "campaign." During the routine operations of the Border Patrol, enforcement of the law is largely a task of that service alone. During a campaign, however, the receiving society extends all available resources, cooperation is established with other policing agencies and in many cases with employers themselves. The end result is a concerted effort (campaign) to repeal an invasion of illegal Mexican aliens.

There have been three significant campaigns initiated by the Border Patrol to tighten up the border. The first occurred in the 1930's, a matter which we have already discussed. The second, which occurred in 1947, is significant to the extent that it was the first of what became a series of campaigns to apprehend illegal Mexican aliens—the forerunner to a pattern of enforcement that resulted in the maximum effort of 1954.

Behind the decision to launch the 1947 campaign were several factors: an unprecedented oversupply of Mexican aliens, an anticipated recession, public indignation over high crime rates along the border, as well as public concern about the "disease infection" potential of the aliens. Starting in California and moving toward Texas, a total of 734 officers were assigned positions on the Mexican border to carry out the 1947 campaign. In March 1947, in less than twenty-five days eight

From El Paso southeast the Rio Grande forms the natural boundary between Mexico and the United States. The U.S. Border Patrol keeps constant watch for "wetbacks" who swim the river as well as those who take overland routes in the area west of El Paso.

Night is the favored time of travel for those who cross on foot. These men were surprised by United States border authorities.

Once he has a job, the wetback farm worker in the border area may smuggle in his family and even enroll children in local schools. This group awaits transportation back to Mexico.

A Patrolman inspects
railway cars at a checkpoint
near the border.

Amalgamated Meat Cutters

Below: A check of this auto
revealed one alien
behind the rear seat.

Official U.S. Border Patrol photo

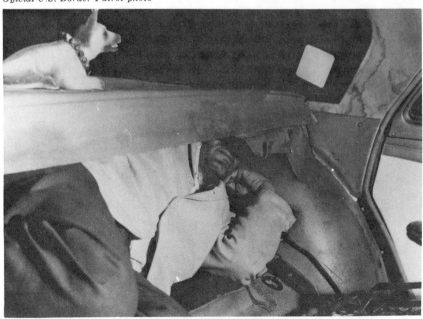

Smuggling can be a very lucrative business. When the tailgates were removed, thirty illegal aliens were discovered in the hidden compartment beneath the packing crates of this truck.

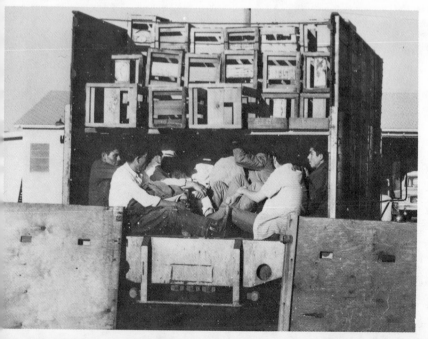

Border Patrol officers apprehended 335 aliens in the Sacramento area ("Operation Sacramento"). Reportedly, this operation involved only five full-time officers who were assisted by three additional officers during the last two weeks (U.S. Department of Justice, I & N Annual Report, 1947:24–25). Proceeding to Fresno, California, 325 aliens were apprehended from April 10 to May 2, 1947 ("Operation Fresno"). "Operation Salinas" effected 322 apprehensions from May 5 through May 29, 1947. "Operation Stockton," lasting from June 2 to June 20, 1947, resulted in the apprehension of 159 aliens.

Swinging over to Texas, more than 117,000 illegal aliens were arrested in the San Antonio district alone, 95 percent of whom were Mexicans (Sanchez and Saunders, 1949:2). As a result of the 1947 campaign, Border Patrol officers apprehended 193,657 deportable aliens, 277 alien smugglers, and 1,020 violators of other laws (U.S. Department of Justice, I & N Annual Report, 1947:24).

In October 1948 the Immigration Service extended its operations to regulate illegal entry on a national level. Until that year the problem was confined to the border states (Leibson, 1949:13). In 1948 a total of 217,555 aliens were expelled from the country. Immigration statistics report 543,538 Mexican illegal aliens apprehended in 1952.

Operation Wetback

By 1954 the Border Patrol had been transformed from a small guard to a small army, and from its inception it has tried to justify its existence as such. Perceiving the role of the Border Patrol, the supervisor of the El Paso district stated:

> The bravery, courage, coolness, and resourcefulness of these patrolmen in times of stress and imminent peril constitute a chapter in the history of the border patrol which does not have its parallel outside of the annals of actual warfare. Conspicuous gallantry and bravery above the call of duty have been displayed by practically every member of the force under circumstances and conditions of defense vastly inferior to those generally obtaining in actual warfare. [U.S. Department of Labor, Annual Report of the Commissioner-General of Immigration, 1925:19]

Thus, the Border Patrol, equipped with all the necessary technological equipment and facilities, was ready to prove itself capable of repelling illegal alien traffic across the border and within the country—an invasion so massive that it prompted one writer to proclaim that, "it often seemed as if the 'whole nation of Mexico' was crossing the border" (Scruggs, 1961:164). Under the leadership of General Joseph May Swing (Commissioner of Immigration and Naturalization), Attorney General Brownwell, and President (General) Eisenhower, whose public service records together range from the 1916 Punitive Invasion of Mexico to the World War II European and Pacific Campaigns, the stage was set for "Operation "Wetback"—an unprecedented campaign to round up an unprecedented number of illegal Mexican aliens (Appendix I; 46). Assisted by federal, state, county, and municipal authorities—including railroad police officers, custom officials, the FBI, and the Army and Navy—and supported by aircraft, watercraft, automobiles, radio units, special task forces, and, perhaps most important of all, public sentiment, including that of growers, the Border Patrol launched the greatest maximum peacetime offensive against a highly exploited, unorganized and unstructured "invading force" of Mexican migrants.

On June 9, 1954, the Attorney General announced that the Border Patrol would begin an operation on June 17, 1954, to rid southern California and western Arizona of "wetbacks" (U.S. Department of Justice, I & N Annual Report, 1954:31). A task force of 800 officers from all Border Patrol sectors were assembled at El Centro and Chula Vista, California. Following a system of blocking off an area and mopping it up, the operation was gradually enlarged until all the industrial and agricultural areas of the entire state of California were secured. The peak in apprehensions was reached during the first week of operations when a daily average of 1,727 illegal aliens were apprehended. Voluntary departures also increased in 1954, according to the Commissioner-General:

> As news of the operation of the Special Force spread, unknown thousands left the country voluntarily to avoid arrest and transfer to the interior of Mexico. Many family groups were encountered and counselled to return to their homes. [U.S. Department of Justice, I & N Annual Report, 1954:32]

It appears that the "fear of God" tactic utilized by the Border Patrol in the 1930's was very much a part of "Operation

Wetback." Reporting on the voluntary departure aspect of the operation, General Swing stated that "these departures were a planned part of the over-all operation and provided a saving to our government" (Swing, 1955:15). By mid-July General Swing's operation swung into action in south Texas. According to the General, all available Immigration and Naturalization Service officer personnel were used in what he called "the maximum effort." These activities were followed by mopping-up operations in the interior and special mobile force units continued to discover aliens in such cities as Spokane, Chicago, Kansas City, and St. Louis, and removed 20,174 illegal Mexican aliens from industrial jobs (U.S. Department of Justice, I & N Annual Report, 1955:14). In 1954, the Commissioner-General reported that in the period from 1944 to 1954, the number of aliens apprehended had increased in volume with nine-tenths of the arrests being Mexicans in lower California, Arizona, and the lower Rio Grande valley in Texas (U.S. Department of Justice, I & N Annual Report, 1954:31). A grand total of 4,961,195 were expelled in that same period. (See Table 4.) By the end of June 1955 the rate of apprehensions had dropped to 11 percent of that of June 1954, and 59 percent of those apprehended were taken into custody within forty-eight hours after crossing the border. According to General Swing:

> The decline in the number of wetbacks found in the United States, even after concentrated efforts were pursued throughout the year, reveals that this is no longer, as in the past, a problem in border control. The border has been secured. To maintain the state of security the Service cannot afford to revert to its operational procedures in effect before the past year. The prevention of illegal entries, as the major ingredient of border control, is more difficult, requires more ingenuity, more men and equipment, but is, in the long run, more economical and more humane than the expulsion process. [U.S. Department of Justice, I & N Annual Report, 1955:14]

It is important, also, to note that the 1947 campaign was reportedly hampered by the lack of detention facilities and the time consumed in collecting wages and personal property of the aliens and in processing the arrest cases. In the first operation of the 1947 campaign, the Assistant Commissioner for Alien Control estimated that only about 25 percent of the officers' time was spent in actually making arrests (U.S. Department of Justice, I & N Annual Report, 1947:25). Looking at the 1954 campaign, particularly the first week of the campaign in which General Swing reported a daily average of 1,727 illegal aliens apprehended, one can only speculate about what speeded up the legal process of issuing warrants, the collection of wages and personal property of the aliens, the processing of arrest cases and the process of deportation—or if indeed these processes occurred at all.

The volume of illegal Mexican entries had continued to increase at a phenomenal rate during the ten-year period from 1944 to 1954. Nevertheless, this influx of illegal Mexican aliens did not seem to concern Congressional authorities—not even the most ardent restrictionists. Yet during this same period three important Congressional acts concerning legal immigration were bitterly debated: (1) the Displaced Persons Act of 1948; (2) the Refugee Act of 1953; and (3) the Immigration and Nationality Act of 1952. Apparently this situation stands out as a social paradox (Hadley, 1956:336). We would add, however, that the situation could best be understood in terms of the desire on the part of many to permit the entry of a certain class of immigrants. Such a desire, nevertheless, is associated with society's ability to regulate the movement. Whereas the Displaced Persons bill, the Refugee bill, and the McCarran-Walter bill involved issues of permanent immigration, the movement of illegal Mexican aliens was probably looked upon as temporary, and, therefore, manageable. Moreover, the movement was probably considered desirable to the extent that the migrants were considered laborers and not settlers. Thus, it would be more fitting to conclude that Congress did not ignore the economic and social consequences, but that Congressional authorities actually sanctioned the movement (Hadley, 1956:339).

In 1952 Congress did take a token step to control the volume of illegal Mexican aliens by passing Public Law 283, making it a felony for importing or harboring illegal aliens. According to Greene, however, this was a limited step: As a concession to agricultural interests, providing employment and the normal practices incident to employment were excluded from punishment under the act (Greene, 1969a:479). Thus it is not a felony to import and harbor illegal aliens for employment, which is one reason we have these illegal border-crossers!

By 1954 the problem of controlling the illegal immigration of Mexican laborers became so serious that Congress was at last forced to hold public hearings. Over the previous ten years *too many* Mexican aliens had come into the country illegally. While Senate Bill 3660 (S. 3660) sought "to make the employment, and related practices, of any alien known by an employer to have entered the United States illegally within three years thereof unlawful . . ." S. 3661 sought "to provide for the seizure and forfeiture of any vessel or vehicle used in the transportation of any alien known by the owner thereof to have entered the United States illegally within three years thereof . . . ." To our knowledge no such bills have been enacted.

1954–1970

The number of illegal Mexican aliens located dropped from 242,608 in 1955 to 30,272 in 1962. The reduction in the number of illegal Mexican aliens may be due to the success of Operation Wetback in effectively removing most of the illegal Mexican aliens that had accumulated over the years. On the other hand, it may reflect a return to the routine procedures of the Border Patrol (termination of the concerted-action approach utilized in 1954 and 1955).

Since 1963 the number of illegal Mexican aliens has continuously increased from 39,124 in 1963 to 201,636 in 1969.° In the entire period from 1924 to 1969, a total of 5,628,712 illegal Mexican aliens were reportedly located by the Immigration and Naturalization Service (4,422,297 before 1955 and 1,206,415 since 1955).

Who Loses?

Two groups lose miserably in the fluctuations which occur on the border: the illegal alien and the domestic farm labor force. The distinction between citizen and illegal alien loses signifi-

---

° While this book was in preparation, the Border Patrol launched a series of new campaigns to apprehend illegal Mexican aliens. These campaigns are similar to earlier campaigns and are currently sources of friction, particularly in Los Angeles, California, and San Antonio, Texas.

cance and becomes a question of peons subordinated to the employer. Describing the situation of the citizen, Sanchez and Saunders wrote:

> No citizen who wants to live in even a minimum of comfort and decency can compete with the wetback wage scale. With an oversupply of cheap, unprotected labor always present, organization of workers is impossible, individual bargaining is futile. There are only two choices: work for what the wetback works for and live as he lives or leave the area. Many accept the former alternative; those who can, choose the second and become displaced persons. [Sanchez and Saunders, 1949:5]

Describing the situation of the Mexican alien in 1948, an El Paso reporter stated:

> From what I saw and heard, not from the workers alone but from patrol inspectors, it was easy to conclude that the black slave of the pre-emancipation years was far better off. Uncle Tom at least had his cabin and a reasonably assured social security. [Leibson, 1949:19]

Reflecting on these descriptions, we can now see how in fact they became prophesies: the condition of the illegal Mexican alien has not changed appreciably. He is still trapped in a subsistence economy. His situation is real and immediate. The exploitation that has been practiced remains one of the most critical processes of domination in the history of twentieth-century United States politics. Both U.S. and Mexican politics have produced this situation by taking advantage of the vulnerable social and economic position of the poor.

Summary and Conclusion

The entry, accumulation, and exploitation of illegal Mexican aliens, including the periodic mass roundups by the Border Patrol, have been closely related to the recruitment practices of agribusiness as well as to its ability to influence policy and law enforcement practices. Adding to this situation has been the indifference of lawmakers toward the traffic of illegal Mexican immigrants as well as toward the effect of this labor on the domestic agricultural labor force, particularly in the Southwest.

As we have indicated, the number of apprehensions of

illegal Mexican aliens in any given year is not necessarily indicative of the volume of illegal entries over the Mexican border for the same year. The decision to "close" the border, whether it be a temporary effort to tighten up enforcement or an extended campaign, has been rather closely related to the relative ability of the receiving society to absorb and profit from the efficient utilization and exploitation of illegal Mexican aliens.

The number of illegal Mexicans reportedly located is particularly significant when compared to legal Mexican immigration. In the last 100 years, no more than 1,525,928 Mexicans were admitted into the United States as legal immigrants. In the twenty-six year period from 1942 to 1968, 5,050,093 Mexican nationals were imported into the United States as temporary contract laborers (braceros). Yet, in the forty-five year period from 1924 to 1969, 5,628,712 illegal Mexican aliens were reportedly located (apprehended) by the United States Immigration and Naturalization Service. Although these figures as reported by the Immigration Service are questionable, perhaps in many cases unreliable, nevertheless they indicate the magnitude of the problem and, when considered in broader terms, suggest the evolution of an immigration policy that may best be understood as an extensive farm labor program— an efficient policy representing a consistent desire for Mexicans as laborers rather than as settlers. This policy stands out as a legitimized and profitable means of acquiring needed labor without incurring the price that characterized the immigration, utilization, and the eventual settlement of European and Oriental immigrants.

iii: *The Invisible People*

It is said that every morning a Mexican lady with a brown paper bag clutched in one hand and her visitor's permit in the other hand will cross the international bridge on her way to the United States. At a designated place she will be picked up by an American housewife driving a late model car and she will be whisked off to the suburbs. She will work as a housemaid all day long for two dollars, and at the end of the day she will be driven back to a place where she can board a bus or trolly and thus return home to Mexico.

Inside the paper bag are a new pair of socks. It is said that if she is stopped in the morning by the immigration officers and questioned, she claims that she is using her visitor's permit to return the socks which she purchased previously and which do not fit. If she is questioned in the evening she can always claim that she had been shopping in the United States during the day and had bought a pair of socks. In the evening, however, she is likely to return with other goods from the United States and therefore may not need the socks to justify her use of the border-crossing permit.

This woman is not a commuter in the strict interpretation of the law, since she does not possess an immigrant visa. In reality she is a commuter because she commutes to her work every day.

She is not a wetback or an illegal immigrant, because she enters the United States legally. She is in fact a legal alien who works illegally in the United States. If and when she is ever caught, and this will be difficult, she can claim that she entered

59

the United States without papers, thus not revealing her border-crossing permit, and she will in all probability be asked if she wants to depart voluntarily from the United States. She will say yes, and a few days later, using the same border-crossing card, she will cross legally into the United States and go back to work illegally. If she is caught doing this two or three times, she may be deported. Deportation means that she will come before a judge, who will notify her of her illegal status and the breaking of the law and who will sentence her to a few years in jail and then suspend the sentence. She will also be told not to come to the United States again to work illegally, because if caught again she will be expected to serve her sentence (Appendix I; 21).

This hypothetical case illustrates a number of points: The ease with which one can cross the border is the first point. The ease with which one can work illegally in the United States is the second point. The third point is the problem presented by an open border and the difficulties which officials face in screening persons who come across the boundary. To be sure this woman could be followed and found working and arrested (with the proper arrest warrants). But when one considers that several thousand other people cross the border every day, the enormity of the problem is easily understood. Without doubt the border can be controlled and controlled effectively, as was illustrated by Project Intercept.* The real question is whether or not the United States is willing to take that action. The answer at the present time seems to be no, and consequently the invisible people by the thousands cross the border every day.

Difficulty in Interviewing

In order to complete our study of the illegal alien we felt that we needed to interview as many aliens as possible. Locating wetbacks in the society at large is a particularly difficult task; interviewing them is next to impossible. Originally we had hoped to interview aliens in a "natural" setting, i.e., before apprehension, rather than in detention centers after apprehension. Our first attempt to do this showed us the folly of our ways.

---

* An attempt, in 1970, to keep out drugs coming from Mexico.

It came to our attention that thirty-two Mexicans were working in an Illinois community of some 15,000 inhabitants. This community is a hundred miles from Chicago and is surrounded by small towns and very rich farmland.

The Mexicans were working in a plant making wheels, earning $2.50 to $3.20 an hour. It must be pointed out that in Mexico the minimum wage is around $2.00 per day, depending on the locality and the type of work. Thus in two days these men were earning as much as they would have earned in Mexico in one month, if they had had a job. To be sure, not all illegals obtain this type of work.

The manager of the plant was interested in having the men learn English so that they could follow simple instructions. In order to accomplish this he arranged to have a teacher from a neighboring town give one-hour lessons to them three days a week. He would release the men for this period of time at the company's expense. The superintendent of schools made a schoolroom available and the program was begun.

We were informed of this arrangement and set about developing a set of questions in order to interview the men. A day before the questionnaire was completed the teacher called to announce that the Immigration and Naturalization Service had staged a raid and had apprehended twenty of the thirty-two Mexican citizens. The other twelve had escaped the dragnet or were here legally (i.e., they had a green card—or immigrant visa—which permits them to work in the United States).

Some weeks later word was received that some of the wetbacks had returned and a Mexican graduate student was sent to the area to interview them. The decision to send a Mexican student was based on the assumption that a fellow citizen, speaking the same language and possessing a similar cultural heritage, would be able to establish rapport with the interviewees more easily than anyone else. Much to our surprise this did not seem to be the case.

The illegal aliens, always in fear of being apprehended, were not eager to be interviewed. They now thought that the teacher had been responsible for calling the immigration authorities. When the teacher tried to set up interviewing appointments for the Mexican student, no one responded favorably because the aliens thought that he was an undercover agent for the Border Patrol. Finally a friend of the teacher's, a wetback whom she assisted on his return from Mexico—a veteran of twenty-two apprehensions—agreed to talk to the student and to respond to a questionnaire. He also put the student in contact with a total of ten other aliens.

Suspicious of Everyone

It soon became clear that the questionnaire must be abandoned. It contained too many questions which were similar to those asked by immigration officials and caused much consternation. As one alien said, "It gives me goose pimples just to think of answering those questions."

The schoolteacher, the veteran wetback, and the interviewer were presumed to be associated with the immigration authorities. No amount of explanation could dispel this association in their minds. Although the aliens lived together in groups of three or four, they claimed to use false names even among themselves because they didn't trust one another. They tried not to reveal their name, place of residence in Mexico, or their legal status in order to protect their families. Most claimed that their documents were in order and that they had entered the country legally. In reality few of them had documents, or if they did, the documents were falsified, which makes their entry illegal.

The interviewees said that most people with whom wetbacks come in contact are suspect, including other aliens, because all are potential informers. It is common knowledge, so they claimed, that the Immigration Service hires Mexicans or Mexican-Americans as special agents to locate wetbacks and turn them in. The officials, they said, also pay a bounty for each alien apprehended.* The officials also work with Mexican postal authorities in selected areas in Mexico. These Mexican officials send the U.S. authorities the return addresses of letters being received from the U.S.; thus it is easy for the U.S. authorities to raid the residences of those sending letters to Mexico who are suspected of being illegal aliens.

The wetback, of necessity, avoids unnecessary contacts with persons not directly associated with his employment and his residence. His range of interaction in the broader community

---

* We were never able to confirm this allegation.

is severely limited, and he lives in constant fear of being turned in by persons around him or of being apprehended by immigration officials either at work, at home, or on the street.

Our interviewer, accompanied by the wetback contact man, approached three aliens in the street and one of them ran away at the first opportunity. When the interviewer was taken into a residence where four aliens lived, the fear was evident in their faces. In this instance one man excused himself to go to the bathroom and did not return during the interview. Another went out the back door and ran away. The other two, convinced that they had been caught, resigned themselves to the situation and agreed to be interviewed.

Fear of Institutions

Places and situations which smack of governmental officialdom are avoided by the Mexican alien. In concrete terms this means banks, postal systems, license bureaus, courts, the police, the church, and unions. It means avoiding places and situations where one might be called upon to produce papers for personal identification. In order to survive, however, one must establish a variety of relationships with other people. Undoubtedly the mere fact that aliens locate in a particular community means that they have or have had some contacts in the community. The matters of employment, housing, cashing checks, buying food and clothing, recreation, etc., all mean establishing relationships with others.

It is in the establishment of these relationships that the wetback becomes vulnerable. An employer, if he bothered to ask the question, could easily find out the citizenship of his employees. What is more important is that he could use this knowledge to his benefit, as could a landlord. We ran into one case where an alien paid another individual five dollars to ten dollars to cash his check. When asked why he didn't go to the bank, he answered that he was frightened by the institution, and besides, having entered into this arrangement he felt sure that he would be turned in by the person who cashed his check if he made other arrangements. In another case an alien had paid fifty dollars for a falsified driver's license. When caught in a minor accident, he was jailed and then deported. The person who reportedly sold him the license, a Mexican-American, then claimed the alien's.car on the grounds that the alien owed him a debt.

In Detention Centers

Because of the difficulties presented we decided to interview aliens after they had been apprehended. We asked for and received permission from the Immigration and Naturalization Service to interview aliens in the three detention centers which they operate. One detention center is located in El Centro, California; another is in El Paso, Texas, and a third is in Los Fresnos, Texas, between Brownsville and Port Isabel. The centers each have facilities to process, house, and feed approximately three hundred persons. Offices for the Border Patrol officers are also located in the centers. The center in Los Fresnos, in addition, is the home of the Border Patrol academy. Each center contains a recreation room and a large *corralón*, or fenced in area, so that the men may enjoy the out-of-doors.

Although we had permission to conduct interviews, these had to be done on a voluntary basis, and there were still other problems to overcome.

Why Tell the Truth?

It is not to the advantage of the wetback to tell the truth when being interviewed—certainly not when being interviewed by the Immigration Service. For one thing the alien wants to make it impossible for the officials of the Immigration Service to determine whether he has been apprehended before. It is almost certain that the names that are given are false ones, that the ages have been somewhat distorted, that the place of birth given is different from the actual place of birth. Another reason for this of course is the fear that something might happen to the family that was left behind. For the same reason and for another, the alien will lie about his place of residence in Mexico. It has been the custom of the detention center to return the Mexican alien to a place in Mexico that is near his place of residence (Appendix I; 28). An alien who admits that he comes from central Mexico will be returned to a place close to his home, if not the actual place. This trip will take several days if transportation is by bus, and it will take many more days for the alien to return to the border in order to cross again. It is therefore much more advantageous for the alien wanting to return to the U.S. to say that he lives in one of the border states or one of the border cities. If this satisfies the authorities he will be sent across the border, and then, of course, his chances for recrossing the border in a short time are very high.*

Most of the wetbacks who are sent back to Mexico are returned voluntarily. That is to say, if he has no criminal record there is no particular reason for keeping the wetback in the U.S. any longer than necessary; it is more efficient and less expensive to return him as quickly as possible, given the facilities available at the detention centers. On the other hand, if an alien admits that he has been apprehended several times, some question is raised and his papers are thoroughly processed, a procedure which takes about two weeks in order to determine whether the alien should be deported. This procedure also involves a hearing before a judge. Thus it is not to the advantage of the Mexican alien to indicate the number of times he has been apprehended, whether he has a criminal record, what kind of documents he used to enter the United States, and whether he plans to return to the United States.

Some officials of the Border Patrol and of the detention centers where we conducted interviews indicated to us that, in general, about 80 percent of what the wetbacks answer them is truth and about 20 percent is not. This statement was made just before one of our interviewing sessions, and it was stated quite emphatically that most people would not tell us where they were actually born if it were other than in the border states, nor would they tell us the actual place of residence, for

* The practice of the Border Patrol, when returning aliens to Mexico, is to charter a Mexican bus for a non-stop trip to the designated destination. The aliens are crossed by bus from the U.S. to Mexico and then herded into the Mexican bus for the trip to the interior. This procedure raises a legal question in our mind: Once an alien is in his own country, what right does the U.S. have to force him into the Mexican bus for a trip he may not want to take?

We found Mexican officials in high and low positions totally ignorant of this practice and denying that it occurs. We also heard of incidents whereby an enterprising bus driver, having deposited the aliens in the interior, then offered the same aliens or other Mexicans a ride back to the border for a nominal fee!

the reasons which we have already stated. The assumption was that most of the interviewees would say that they were born in a border state and that they resided in a border state or a border city. It was also thought that most of the aliens would tell us this was their first apprehension and that they would not tell us that they planned to return to the United States. At the end of the day, to our surprise, few people claimed that they were born or that they lived in border states, many of them indicated that they had been apprehended several times, and almost all of them indicated that they would return to the United States soon. Evidently, then, we were not perceived as official agents of the Immigration and Naturalization Service, in spite of the fact that we were using their premises for our interviews.

Who Should Interview?

From what has been said so far, it follows that interviewing illegal aliens in the society at large presents a number of difficulties. For the most part they live in fear of being turned in, in fear of being apprehended; they can trust few people and are suspicious of most. They have little recourse to established institutions and, of course, live outside of the legal structures. They are subject to exploitation, a condition which few can escape.

The ideal person to interview this population, then, is not easily identified. A fellow Mexican, even a fellow wetback is no more free of suspicion than a Mexican-American or an Anglo.

Most people who *seek* them out are associated with officialdom. Once the aliens have been apprehended and placed in the detention centers, however, it is not difficult to interview them on a voluntary basis. They have little to do, the days are long and hot, and diversion is welcomed by most. Besides all this, being interviewed in a detention center is simply to be expected.

Other Methodological Problems

Every study which hopes to make generalizations about its findings tries to establish what we call the universe of study. Once having established the universe, careful samples are drawn which represent this universe.

In our case the universe of study logically should be all

illegal Mexican aliens in the United States, but no one knows how many there are nor where they are located.

The number of illegals apprehended is the next possible universe from which to sample. The problem presented here is that the number of apprehensions do not necessarily represent the number of *individuals* apprehended. Nor does it represent the number of individuals who have come into the United States. Some individuals have been apprehended as many as twenty-two times in four or five years, others only once. Some have been apprehended three times in the same day. Our interviewer spoke to two individuals in one of the detention centers who had worked on the grounds at the University of Notre Dame. When the wetbacks learned of his university affiliation, they immediately wanted to talk more. The interviewer said, "You *used* to work at the University?" They answered, "No, no, we *work* at the University," implying that they were suffering a temporary inconvenience for having been apprehended in a neighboring town but that they would soon return to work.

Theoretically a universe could be established of all those people who pass through the detention centers. There would be many duplications over a period of time, one individual with several false names, etc. Then, too, individuals sometimes spend as little as four hours in the centers while being processed and returned to Mexico. Others spend a few days; others, particularly those to be deported or to be sent to a federal prison, may spend several weeks in the center.

The records of the three detention centers, during a given time period, could serve as a universe. These records, however, suffer from the same deficiencies discussed above.

Since the universe is difficult to establish, drawing a sample representing this universe is equally difficult. All interviews, by official edict, must be on a voluntary basis. Thus refusals would play havoc with attempts at sampling. Then, too, the number of wetbacks in any given center in any given day varies between 100 and 300.

We finally settled for the following: Instead of attempting a representative sample of a universe we would spend three days in each center. Instead of a lengthy interview (because of the great turnover in each center each day), we would administer a questionnaire to as many persons as possible. Realizing that many wetbacks would be illiterate, we arranged for some assistance while administering the questionnaire. In this manner we reached 493 men of an estimated 1,000 in the three centers at the time of the questioning. Many were also interviewed in depth. A careful effort was made to get those who presumably had been apprehended only once and passed through the centers quickly, as well as those who were repeaters and/or were being deported.

We think our data are reasonably accurate for a number of reasons. Since the wetbacks had already been apprehended and processed by the Immigration authorities in the detention centers, presumably they had been asked all of the official questions that they were going to be asked before being sent back to Mexico. We then followed with many questions which were similar to those that had already been asked them (age, place of birth, place of residence), but also included many questions which were of interest to them and which had not previously been asked. Our interviewer was a Mexican who assured them that he was not associated with the Immigration Service but rather with a Catholic university in the North and that this study was being done to ascertain some of the problems being confronted by the illegal Mexican immigrant.

It was made very clear in many ways that we were not associated with the Immigration Service but that the Immigration Service was permitting us to use their facilities in order to gather information for a broader study.

Many of the more literate Mexicans offered to help the less literate Mexicans during the completion of the questionnaire. The cooperation which was given to us by the wetbacks was considerable.

After the questionnaire had been answered, the interviewer asked if anyone wanted to stay to discuss questions of interest to him, and invariably most of those completing the questionnaire stayed around to discuss the general problems of wetbacks in the United States.

Some of the immigration authorities, as indicated earlier in this chapter, told us not to expect the truth on about 20 percent of the responses, in particular those questions dealing with place of residence, place of birth, number of times apprehended, and whether or not they planned to return to the United States. We found that the answers to these questions were contrary to the expectations of the immigration officials, thus leading us to believe that we were getting truthful answers.

Our most persuasive argument for giving us the truth was apparently our great stress upon the confidentiality of the data and the anonymity of the respondent. The immigration officials of necessity must take names, fingerprints, and other necessary information. We emphasized the fact that we did not want their names, precisely because we did not want to be able to identify them. This respect for their privacy and the prospect of complete anonymity appeared to convince them that we were no threat.

In order to check on the validity of the information given us in these interviews, we decided that a participant observer might be used. A Mexican graduate student participating in our research agreed to disguise himself as a wetback. Chapter VII presents his personal account.

iv: *The Game*

On the morning of August 2, 1969, the Immigration and Naturalization Service was contacted by the Illinois State Police, advising them that they had detained an alleged U.S. citizen who was accompanied by a group of six Mexican aliens. Investigators were dispatched to the exit on Interstate 55 to highway 294 (near Hinsdale, Illinois), where all subjects were interviewed.

The interrogation revealed that the smuggler had contacted the aliens on July 25, 1969, at a hotel, Casa de Huespedes, in Miguel Alemán, Tamaulipas, Mexico. At that time they discussed transportation to Chicago, but no arrangements were made. Later they contacted the smuggler in a restaurant in Miguel Alemán where all arrangements were made for their transportation to Chicago. They agreed that they would each pay $200 for his assistance. They were told by the smuggler that they should go to Ciudad Mier and stay overnight. The aliens caught a bus to Ciudad Mier and there they rented one room for the night at the Hotel Colonial. They were picked up by the smuggler on the morning of July 29, 1969, and transported to a house near the Rio Grande. The smuggler then told the aliens that the man who lived in that house would lead them to the river and show them exactly where to cross.

Later they were escorted to the river and they entered the United States illegally at about 3:00 P.M. on July 29, 1969. They hid in the brush as they were instructed to do, and after dark the same day the smuggler came to their hiding place and led them to a house close to the river which he identified as his own. They stayed in this house until the early morning of July 30, 1969. Before departing from the house each of the aliens paid $25 to the smuggler and promised to pay the remaining $175 after their arrival in Chicago. The aliens then boarded a pickup truck and drove to Levelland, Texas, where they stayed overnight. The next day they boarded another pickup, which took them to a small town in Oklahoma where they spent the night. The following day they left that house and traveled until they were caught by the Illinois State Police on highway 294.

They had been instructed that, in the event of being stopped by the immigration officers, they should say that they had been hitchhiking and the driver had given them a ride and was not receiving any pay for it. They were also instructed to say that they had entered the United States on July 23, 1969, when in fact they had entered on July 29. The aliens and the smuggler were turned over to the proper authorities for prosecution.

Many cases are similar to this one. From our interviews with wetbacks at the detention centers we learned of some of their patterns of movement and behavior and of the steps which they may take before crossing, while crossing, and after crossing the border.

One day a young Mexican decides the time has come to leave his village. He has heard the stories of others' experiences. He recognizes the hardships—yet, he has no job, his parents or his wife and children must be taken care of, or perhaps he wants to get married. His choice, since there is no work in the village, is either to move to the city—Guadalajara or Mexico City—or to move to the northern border.

In the interior of Mexico it is said that much work is available in the U.S. Everyone knows that the braceros made out well, and although the Bracero Program no longer exists, U.S. employers are eager for good laborers and almost anyone can get work if he can cross the border. There are a few technicalities involved however: One must get an immigrant visa if he is to work in the U.S. and perhaps live in Mexico; or one must get a border-crossing permit in order to cross the bridges; or one may sneak across the border, taking the chance of getting caught. None of these methods are without problems, and they all cost money.

Unless the young man lives in the border area, he will face, at some point in his decision-making process, the problem of the cost of the trip to the U.S. In order to get the money for the trip he might sell a piece of land or a cow, or he might leave something valuable as collateral for a loan. In the latter case he will have to pay a monthly interest rate of 10 to 15 percent on the amount borrowed.

If he gets the money for the trip, he may look for a local agent or just an informant who will put him in contact with a *pasador*. Arrangements will be made for the *pasador* to meet him at some Mexican border town. Depending on the formality of the deal with the local agent or informant, the would-be alien will probably pay for this first service (usually a small fee from ten pesos to a hundred pesos). Or he may be charged a part of the total price agreed upon for smuggling him to the U.S. The local agent will give him an address, usually of a hotel in a Mexican border town where he will be contacted by the *pasador*.

If the would-be alien is lucky enough to have friends or relatives in the U.S., he might obtain a tourist visa in any U.S. consulate and fly to some point in the U.S., preferably a place removed from the border area, where he will pass as a tourist. If he arouses suspicion by his appearance, he might be requested to exhibit the money that he will spend while visiting in the U.S. After passing the immigration inspection he will be welcomed by his friend or relative, who will get a job for him someplace in Los Angeles or Chicago. In this case he will have legally entered the U.S., but will become illegal, that is, a wetback, as soon as he begins to work.

If the young man has no contacts either on the Mexican border or in the U.S., he may go to a border city on his own and begin walking around the main square (*plaza principal*) or along the river in search of *pasadores* or *enganchadores*, who will smuggle him to the U.S. and perhaps even arrange a job for him. He might go to a bar and find someone selling false documents to use in crossing the border. Or he may try to find someone who will help him apply for a "green card."

The cost of the trip to the U.S. varies according to the place of departure and the destination.

If the Mexican lives in central Mexico—for example, Guanajuato—he will need as much as 1,500 pesos (120 U.S. dollars). He will spend most of the money in the U.S. while looking for a job and the rest will go to a smuggler who will charge him for a "safe" crossing of the border. But if the alien lives in Guanajuato and wants to go as far as Chicago he will need 320 U.S. dollars for expenses for the journey.

If the would-be illegal alien cannot raise the money for the trip to the U.S., he will hitchhike to a Mexican border town and keep alert for those groups who are talking about crossing illegally (*"de mojado"*). There is no reason to talk secretly about crossing, since there is no apparent concern on the part of Mexican authorities to prevent the illegal crossing. It will be relatively easy to find those groups planning the crossing for that night. Once together they will all follow the person who claims to know the best place for crossing, based upon past experiences.

The illegal crossing, whether made with the aid of a smuggler or otherwise, usually takes place during the night, not only because it is easier to hide in the darkness, but because there must be plenty of time to look for a job once in the U.S. or else to advance as far as possible from the border, going northward, in order to avoid the zone in which the Border Patrol is more active.

Both Border Patrol officials and wetbacks agree that the farther north from the border a wetback goes, the less the probabilities of being caught. Why, then, would a wetback stop in the border zone looking for a job? The answer we have gathered from our interviews is that the wetback who has crossed without money may be starving after a long journey from his home town and in urgent need of work and money.

If the wetback wants to advance north, toward the industrial areas of the Midwest, he must cross that border zone where the Border Patrol is active as quickly as possible, so he must carry enough food and water for a journey of three days of walking by night and sleeping by day. Quite often the wetback who does not have enough food and water for the long journey has to seek out the Border Patrol, who will apprehend him and feed him; or he may try to find food regardless of the risk of being caught.

If a Mexican enters for the first time as a wetback and does not have contacts in the U.S., it is likely that he will look for a job in agriculture. The reasons for this seem to be that (1) the majority of wetbacks come from rural areas in Mexico, and therefore agriculture is what they know; (2) agriculture in the U.S. border area seems to be a place where a certain amount of socialization takes place, particularly in such things as how to behave and what places and circumstances to avoid if one wants to get away from the Border Patrol. In short, agriculture seems to be the place where the newcomer learns about the unwritten code of wetback behavior.

The Contacts

Mexican illegals wishing to enter the U.S. to work make contact in this country in a variety of ways. The most common way is through relatives and friends who reside here. In the border region former employers are common contacts.

Our experience in northern Indiana and northern Illinois suggests that relatives and friends who are already here advise wetbacks, by mail or courier, of employment opportunities. The great majority of the wetbacks we interviewed could neither speak nor understand English. It is therefore remarkable that they are able to make their way north and survive. It is not really necessary to know English along the border and in cities with high concentrations of people who speak Spanish, such as San Antonio, Los Angeles, San Francisco, Albuquerque, but not knowing English is a great handicap in the rest of the country, although it is true that many midwestern, northern, and eastern communities now have sizable groups of people who speak Spanish (Mexican-Americans, Puerto Ricans, Cubans, and others).

Another contact is suggested and that is the smuggler. He is necessary particularly for the purpose of getting away from the border area as quickly as possible. He is also very expensive. Recent cases reported indicated that the cost for being smuggled and transported away from the border was $200 to $300. In this instance the men were apprehended within five minutes of being dropped off. Two prominent lawyers in Texas insist that the Border Patrol admits that if they did not have informants among the smugglers, they (the Patrol) could not apprehend the numbers that they do with the staff available.

An official of the Border Patrol admitted to this writer that they did maintain Mexican "spies" in the Mexican border towns who were very useful and helpful. This practice was confirmed by a wetback who in a group interview was trying to convey the idea that the spy for the Border Patrol should not be blamed as a traitor. He told of the situation of one of his cousins who was caught while working for a good salary and who was told by the Border Patrol that in order to avoid apprehension and to keep his job he would have to "turn in" a quota of wetbacks weekly. In these circumstances, he continued, "it is very difficult to be a hero." Some wetbacks knew about the system of informants and added heaven help the informant if his name were ever found out!

The smuggler can also be very dangerous. The hardships and hazards encountered by the wetback are such that in some instances even death is the price paid, as reported in the opening case in the Introduction. Another danger lies in the system reported to us whereby the illegal is loaned money by the smuggler at extremely high interest rates, for the expenses incurred in entering the U.S. He is then threatened that if the money is not repaid the family left behind will be injured and held accountable. The wetback who borrows, say $150 (1,875 pesos), makes it to Los Angeles, and is apprehended before he finds a job and then is returned to Mexico must begin the process all over again. If he finds a well-paying job the second time, he may be able to pay his debts before the next apprehension. If he is apprehended again and remains in Mexico, it will be years before he can pay off the debt, given the unemployment conditions and the wage structures in Mexico.

What we call the independents are those individuals who come across singly or in twos or threes to try to find employment, usually agricultural, just miles across the border. These persons usually do not have any contacts in the U.S., nor do they bother with the smuggling system. Now and again some of these individuals are found wandering in circles in the deserts, lost and without water. Sometimes they are found dead.

Documents

Legal documents include a tourist card limited to a certain time period, a border passing permit restricted in time (usually seventy-two hours) and distance, or an immigrant visa. (See Appendix I; 1, 31, 35.)

Some wetbacks obtain a tourist card, enter legally, get a job, and do not return until apprehended, at which time they claim to have no papers. One situation has come to our attention whereby a small group of Mexicans posing as tourists obtain a tourist card for entering the U.S. legally. They take a plane to Chicago (cheaper than paying smugglers), and then a bus to the small town in Indiana where they all work.

On a recent trip from Mexico City to Chicago we were seated near a Mexican citizen who was dressed in the type of clothes that one can see at a wedding fiesta in a peasant community. He was about thirty-five years old, and we learned later that he came from a small town in Michoácan. Upon arriving at the airport we followed him closely and offered to act as interpreters, since he did not speak English.

His documentation was a tourist card. When an immigration official asked where he was going to stay he answered, "por ahi nomas" [here and there—anywhere]. When asked how long he planned to stay in the U.S. he answered, "pos nomas unos cuantos dias" [just a few days].

The lack of definiteness in his answers aroused the suspicion of the interrogating official and he was sent to yet another official, who, among other things, asked him to show the amount of money he was going to spend in the U.S., whereupon the man produced $200 and the return trip ticket. Since airlines have had to return persons who are not admitted to the U.S., they now demand that the tourist purchase a round-trip ticket.

Having passed inspection, the alien told us that he had come to Chicago to live with a cousin, whom he did not want to implicate during the interrogation. At his request we called the cousin, who was to come to the airport shortly. We were then asked how he could get a refund for his return trip ticket, because that was the only source of funds for his living expenses. As to the $200, that was money that a friend of his had given him to pay a debt that the friend owed to a relative in Chicago.

We were told that the man's cousin had a job for him in Chicago and he planned to work long enough to save $800 in order to buy land in his home town.

This tourist will become a wetback when he begins working. When apprehended he will claim to have entered the U.S. without inspection and without papers.

Sometimes an American citizen, usually a Mexican-American, will offer to marry a Mexican for a price of $200 to $300, to be paid over a two-year period. The idea behind this arrangement is twofold. It will permit the alien to enter the U.S. as a husband of an American citizen and it will place him high in priority for obtaining legal documents to enter the U.S. as an immigrant. We were unable to determine how widespread this practice is, but it is one way of entering the U.S. The informant told us that to his knowledge the couple live together for one or two years and then they separate or become divorced, thus ending the relationship. (See Appendix I; 31, 35.)

Falsified documents are of several kinds: visas, commuter cards, passports, and permits for visiting, shopping, and pleasure. These may be made by the individuals, but more generally they are purchased. These falsified documents, according to our interviews, are rather easily detected and not widely used by wetbacks.

Illegal documents consist of those legal documents purchased from someone else. For example, if relatives or friends of approximately the same age have such documents and are willing to rent or sell them, this is easily done. When individuals possessing legal documents die, relatives will either use them themselves or sell them to others.

American citizens—mostly Mexican-Americans—who live on the border or who are visiting across the border may sell their birth certificate or baptismal certificate and, on return to the U.S., replace it with a new one. (See Appendix I; 27.)

Among those whom we interviewed the great majority (82 percent) admitted to having entered without inspection and without papers. (See Table 5.)

Walk, Swim, or Ride

The most common way of crossing the border appears to be by walking. The land boundary stretches from El Paso, Texas, west to the Pacific Ocean. This includes the boundaries of New Mexico, Arizona, and California. Some of this area is fenced, some is not. When illegal aliens climb the fence or cut it, they are sometimes called *alambristas*. The term *wetback*, however, is in more general usage, whether one walks or swims.

Some people cross at the international bridge but only if

TABLE 5

Type of Document Used to Enter United States

Document	Number	Percent
No answer	18	3.65
Green card	25	5.07
Visitor's card	12	2.43
Visa	5	1.01
False papers	27	5.48
Without papers	406	82.35
Total	493	99.99

they have some documents. Most walk across at some point where they feel detection will be less likely. The best time to enter is at dusk when there is less likelihood of being seen and there is the dark of night ahead for walking.

The Border Patrol maintains a wide drag strip in some parts of the border along the U.S. side, which is maintained daily. This strip is wide enough that individuals cannot jump across it and wetbacks invariably leave tracks (footprints) when they come across. In early morning a light airplane will pick up the tracks and notify the nearest officers on patrol. This tracking system is evidently most efficient, as suggested by the evidence. A great number of those aliens interviewed were apprehended before they found a job and a large number had been in the U.S. only "days" before being apprehended.

From El Paso southeast to the Gulf of Mexico the international boundary is the Rio Grande. One swims or wades or rides a boat across the river. Depending on the place and the time of year, swimming may be dangerous and there are accounts of persons drowning while attempting to cross. Smugglers will ferry people across, generally for four dollars, for those who can't swim or if the river is too deep for wading. Among those whom we interviewed, the majority crossed the border by walking or swimming, which immediately suggests that they entered without papers and without inspection. Those who entered by either bus, car, train, or plane most likely had legal, illegal, or falsified documents. (See Table 6.)

Once in the U.S. the game is intensified and the problem is one of getting to the destination as quickly as possible without detection. The safest way of getting into the interior is by air-

TABLE 6

METHOD OF CROSSING THE BORDER

Method	Number	Percent
No answer	6	1.22
On foot	313	63.49
Swimming	111	22.52
By boat	1	.20
By car	44	8.92
By train	6	1.22
By plane	2	.41
By bus	10	2.03
Total	493	100.00

plane, because this implies a tourist card and the alien is safe for some time. From the border to the destination by taxi or private car is the next safest method. The probability of being stopped and questioned by the Border Patrol is not as great. Using the train and the bus is least safe because these public conveyances are checked regularly, as are the depots and terminals.

Some illegal aliens whom we interviewed signed up with U.S. fishing boats immediately upon crossing into the U.S. near the Gulf and went off to sea. When the fishing vessels come into port, however, the aliens are quickly picked up because the boats and the crews are inspected.

There may be other ways of making contacts and arrangements, of securing documents, and of crossing the international boundary in order to work in the U.S. What is presented here is what we learned from interviewing wetbacks in the North and in detention centers, and from interviews with officials of the Immigration and Naturalization Service.

v: Where Did You Go and What Did You Do?

Apprehensions During the Past Few Years

At the present time illegal entries of Mexicans are on the increase. The peak was in 1954 when, during "Operation Wetback," over a million were apprehended, and during this period the Bracero Program was operating. The apprehension of illegals declined considerably during the next few years, 242,608 in 1955, 72,442 in 1956, and 29,651 in 1960. Since the end of the Bracero Program, 1964, there has been a gradual increase of the wetback apprehensions, from 43,844 in 1964 to 201,636 in 1969.

As has been said before, the Bracero Program was an "ideal" solution to labor demands in agriculture from the employer's viewpoint. Since these were single individuals, no housing for families was necessary; wages and other considerations favorable to agribusiness were established; and much of the program was subsidized by the federal government and administered by state employment agencies. In this program the only persons who were in a disadvantaged position were domestic agricultural workers (U.S. citizens) willing to work (but for decent wages) and the Mexican nationals.

Some persons, including immigration and naturalization officials, suggest that the increase of wetbacks in the past five-year period is due to the termination of the Bracero Program. However, other factors seem to provide a more reasonable explanation: (1) the U.S. economy demands cheap labor, particularly in agriculture; (2) the border region has always been and continues to be a magnet for Mexicans; (3) the rate of

TABLE 7

DEPORTABLE MEXICAN ALIENS FOUND IN U.S. BY TIME AND STATUS
WHEN APPREHENDED, FISCAL YEAR, 1968

	Adult Males	Women and Children	Total°
Number	133,024	18,681	151,705
Time When Apprehended			
At entry	26,738	3,035	29,773
Within 72 hours	25,199	5,886	31,085
4–30 days	39,710	3,729	43,439
1–6 months	32,750	3,477	36,227
7 months –1 year	4,678	957	5,635
Over 1 year	3,924	1,597	5,521
Status When Found			
Employment			
In agriculture	39,938	1,488	41,426
Industry & other	26,055	5,375	31,430
Seeking employment	54,310	5,118	59,428
Other			
In institutions	5,221	895	6,416
In travel	55,747	7,899	63,646

SOURCE: Monthly reports (Form G-23.18), unpublished material, Immigration and Naturalization Service, 1968.

° Percentages were not calculated because of the inconsistency of these figures with other published figures from the same source.

population increase in Mexico for the last two generations has been phenomenal; (4) Mexico has not been able to keep up with this population growth despite tremendous efforts in economic growth. Thus unemployment continues on the increase.

If the termination of the Bracero Program is responsible for the increase in wetbacks in 1969, why is it that in 1954, when the Bracero Program was in full swing, 309,033 braceros were admitted and 1,075,168 wetbacks were apprehended? As long as Mexico cannot provide adequately for its population and unemployment continues to be a problem, as long as the border remains relatively open and accessible over hundreds of miles, as long as the Border Patrol remains at its present strength, as long as the border region demands cheap labor, and as long as illegal aliens *and their U.S. employers* are not

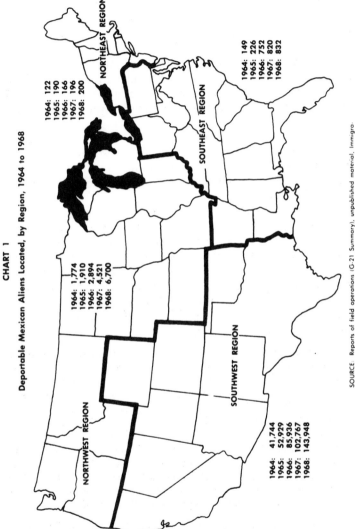

CHART 1

Deportable Mexican Aliens Located, by Region, 1964 to 1968

NORTHEAST REGION

1964: 122
1965: 190
1966: 166
1967: 196
1968: 200

1964: 149
1965: 226
1966: 752
1967: 820
1968: 832

SOUTHEAST REGION

1964: 1,774
1965: 1,910
1966: 2,894
1967: 4,521
1968: 6,700

SOUTHWEST REGION

NORTHWEST REGION

1964: 41,744
1965: 52,929
1966: 85,936
1967: 102,767
1968: 143,948

SOURCE: Reports of field operations (G-21 Summary), unpublished material, Immigration and Naturalization Service, for each fiscal year.

penalized for participating in this traffic, we will always have wetbacks and the numbers will continue to increase rather than diminish.

The great majority of wetbacks are males; most are apprehended fairly close to the border or at least in those states bordering Mexico. They are seldom in the U.S. for any great length of time before being apprehended and most are apprehended while looking for work or while traveling. Of those who are working, the majority work in agriculture. Table 7 and Chart 1 suggest the magnitude of the problem in recent years.

In 1968 over 151,000 Mexican aliens were apprehended in the U.S. Of these very close to 144,000 were apprehended in the Southwest region. The apprehensions are shown in Table 8 by states. (See Appendix II for a map of both regional and district boundaries.)

These data on a national scale show that most of the wetbacks are apprehended in the four states bordering Mexico. Our own data reveal the same situation. A third of our respondents were apprehended within hours or days after crossing the border and before they were employed. Another third worked for the first time and were caught in Texas. The other third worked for the first time and were caught in California (13%), Arizona (12%), New Mexico (6%), Colorado (.7%), and other western states (.8%).

> The U.S. is not and has never been a very significant "vent for Mexico's surplus population" or a "labor escape valve" as others have claimed. Only some 3% (1.5 million) of the total immigration to the United States since 1820 (44.0 million) has come from Mexico. Only 5.7% (6,044) of the aliens naturalized in 1967 (104,902) came from Mexico. In 1967 41,271 people immigrated from Mexico into the U.S. and the U.S. Department of State immigration projections for 1969 are down to 24,300. Assuming that Mexico's population is currently increasing at about one and one half million persons per year, the U.S. receives only about 2% of the total annual population increase, hardly a significant vent of surplus population. [Price, 1969:17]

We thoroughly disagree with this position. In the first place Professor Price is considering only legal immigration to support his position. He has neglected to consider the millions of braceros, the millions of wetbacks, and the thousands of com-

TABLE 8

APPREHENSION OF MEXICAN ALIENS IN THE SOUTHWEST
REGION BY STATE, 1968

Location	Number
U.S. total	151,680
Southwest Region Total	143,948
California:	71,824
Los Angeles	20,766
San Francisco	2,721
Chula Vista	23,963
El Centro	8,167
Livermore	16,207
Texas:	59,583
El Paso	21,506
Del Rio	9,562
Marfa	8,811
Laredo	5,678
Port Isabel	5,386
McAllen	4,979
San Antonio	3,661
Arizona:	11,362
Yuma	5,970
Tucson	4,470
Phoenix	922
Colorado:	
Denver	1,177
Hawaii:	
Honolulu	2

SOURCE: Reports of Field Operations (G-21 Summary), unpublished
material, Immigration and Naturalization Service, 1968.

muters who have been in and out of the U.S. labor force. If
for any given year one were to compile statistics of all of the
Mexicans who work (legally and illegally) in the U.S. and
compare those figures with the number of new jobs that Mexico was unable to provide to keep up with its population
growth, the numbers working in the U.S. would be a significant proportion of that number of new jobs that Mexico was
unable to provide.

Our data suggest that the pattern of migration for the alien is related to the economic conditions in Mexico. In general, we can say that the movement of people from the rural areas to the urban areas during the past few years has been phenomenal. Obviously the larger cities have attracted the most migrants. The two major areas of concentration of this internal migration, however, have been the Federal District and the northern border region. Mexico City has grown by leaps and bounds but at a slower rate of growth than the border cities. The tremendously high population growth for the nation as a whole (fourth in the world) gives impetus to the internal population shifts. Over the years, then, the border region has grown at an accelerated pace, piling up the poor in the several cities adjacent to the United States.

With the piling up of the poor in Mexican border cities and with so many unemployed, it is only natural that they will attempt to cross the border for work in order to survive.

We suspect that on their first attempt to enter the U.S. illegally, most will be apprehended within a relatively short time, but they will have gained much experience in the intricacies of border crossing.

Since the Border Patrol is most effective along the border, the alien, on his next crossing, will attempt to move as far north as possible. Other compelling reasons for this, besides the concentration of border officers along the border are the better wages in the North, are the opportunity to work in non-agricultural occupations, and less exploitation.

If, on the second attempt, the alien is apprehended close to the border and before finding employment, his third attempt to enter the U.S. is likely to be more sophisticated, more expensive, and involve more people. It is at this time that the smuggling operation is contacted. The smuggling of bodies from Mexico to the U.S. is a big business, involving people on both sides of the border. In the El Paso sector along, in 1965, there were 114 cases of smuggling, involving 317 aliens and 130 principals (or persons assisting). Seventy of the principals were detained. In the first ten months of 1969 there were 439 cases, involving 2,108 aliens and 534 principals, 355 of whom were detained (U.S. Border Patrol, November 13, 1969, unpublished).

Referring to our data on apprehension, the variation between our sample and the more general figures is not great.

TABLE 9
NUMBER OF TIMES APPREHENDED

Number	Number	Percent
At least once	265	53.75
Twice	103	20.89
Three times	51	10.34
Four times	35	7.10
Five times	15	3.04
Six times	8	1.62
Seven times	4	.81
Eight to twelve times	7	1.42
Thirteen to sixteen times	1	.20
Over seventeen times	4	.81
Total	493	99.98

Most of the individuals in our sample (n = 493) were apprehended on the street (50%) or in a public place (9%). Many were apprehended at work (26%) or at home (11%), the latter figure suggesting that they were already established and working. A slight variation between our data and the national data is related to the question of employment. Table 7 indicates that almost 50% of those apprehended in 1968 were working. Our data indicate that 51% had employment when they were apprehended. The data in Table 7 also indicate that the great majority of the aliens were in the U.S. illegally a relatively short time, the great majority under six months. We asked our respondents how long they had been away from Mexico and received similar answers. Sixty per cent had been away from one to six months. Only 22 (out of 493) had been away from Mexico more than a year. For the nation, in 1968, 5,521 (out of 151,705) aliens had been in the U.S. illegally over one year.

On a national level, it is difficult to compile accurate statistics as to the number of times that a person has been apprehended, for the reasons mentioned in Chapter III. Since our interviews were held in detention camps, obviously all of our interviewees had been caught once. Some admitted to having been caught twice (21%), 10% said they had been caught three times, and 15% had been caught between four and eighteen times. (See Table 9.)

Here a word should be added about the significance of the

statistics on apprehensions. At a conference held at the University of California at Davis, on April 11, 1970, immigration officials stated that the number of apprehensions is directly related to their manpower available in a given area. This suggests that if more patrolmen were available in the U.S., there would be more apprehensions. If more were available in the North, more aliens would get caught. Some Border Patrol officers also estimate that three illegal entrants are undetected for every one that is caught (Greene, 1969a:479). At best these are unofficial, individual guesses and therefore not very reliable.

Nevertheless we must be dealing with a sizable population, in spite of the fact that many of those apprehended have been apprehended two or three times. This becomes more significant when one considers that the apprehensions in 1969 were over 200,000 and in the first quarter of 1970 it appeared that there was a 30% increase over 1969.

vi: A Profile of Aspirations and Desperation

The wetback who only violates the immigration law does not consider himself a criminal or lawbreaker. He is playing a game, trying to outwit the authorities. To be sure the stakes are high (his survival), but there are few sanctions. If he stays clear of the drug traffic, stealing, drunkeness, fighting, etc., that is if he doesn't violate local, state, or other federal laws, the worst that can happen to him, when apprehended, is a trip to one of the detention centers (sometimes by commercial plane, for example, from Denver), a short stay there, uniformly good treatment as far as we could ascertain, and then a bus trip to Mexico. The whole procedure is quite an inconvenience, more so if the individual plans to return to his job. Even when deported or when caught again after being deported, the judges tend to be lenient and suspend a large part of each sentence. If this were not so, our federal prisons would be overcrowded.

Demographic Considerations

In most populations the most mobile segment is usually represented by the young adults. The wetbacks whom we interviewed are no exception to this observation. Seventy-one percent of the interviewees were under 30 years of age. Of the total, 19% were under 20 and 32% were between 21 and 25 years of age. These statistics are consistent with those reported by Saunders and Leonard (1951), and Hadley (1956).

When we compare their present age with their age at first entry, however, we find that the majority of the aliens entered the U.S. at a very young age. (See Table 10.)

TABLE 10

AGE DISTRIBUTION OF THOSE INTERVIEWED AND THEIR AGE
AT FIRST ENTRY INTO THE U.S.

Age	Those Interviewed		Their Age at First Entry	
	No.	%	No.	%
No answer	4	.81	26	5.27
Under 20 years	93	18.86	184	37.32
21–25 years	157	31.85	182	36.92
26–30 years	99	20.08	57	11.56
31–35 years	51	10.34	18	3.65
36–40 years	48	9.74	13	2.64
41–45 years	24	4.87	5	1.01
46–50 years	10	2.03	7	1.42
51–55 years	5	1.01	1	.20
Over 56 years	2	.41	0	.00
Total	493	99.99	493	99.99

Although all of the aliens whom we interviewed were males, a small percentage of the aliens who are apprehended are women and children. Unskilled women, of course, can work in a variety of jobs in agriculture, as dishwashers in restaurants, as hotel maids, in custodial jobs, as housemaids, and in some service occupations.

Becoming a wetback, however, has been more the role of the male, since it entails long journeys, working with groups of men, hard labor, and a dangerous undertaking. In spite of this, Saunders and Leonard (1951) report 16% of those in their survey were females and the 1968 figures from the Immigration and Naturalization Service show 12%.

Forty-six percent of our interviewees were single as compared to 60% of those reported by Saunders and Leonard (1951). Forty percent were legally married, 8% were living in free union, and the rest (22 individuals) were widowed, divorced, or separated.

With regard to education more than 90% had completed less than six grades. Twenty-eight percent had never been to school, 5% had completed high school, and 3% had gone beyond high school.

As one might expect almost 90% could neither speak nor

understand English. Five percent could understand English, 3% could understand and speak, and 1.6% could understand, speak, and write English.

Of those interviewed 54 or 11% had one to three children born in the U.S. Twenty-five percent had relatives who were born in the U.S., of whom most are still U.S. citizens. Thirty-eight percent had relatives (citizens and non-citizens) in the U.S. The years of U.S. residence for 22% of the aliens was between one and nine years. We are dealing, then, with a group that has had considerable experience within the U.S. in spite of their general inability to speak the language. Twenty-eight percent had been members of the Bracero Program. Fifty-four percent had been apprehended at least once, 21% at least twice, and one-fourth admitted to being apprehended between three and seventeen times. Four persons said that they were apprehended over 17 times.

The questions on employment revealed that the majority (57%) had been employed in Mexico in agriculture. Only 12% had been employed in skilled work. In the U.S., of those who were employed when apprehended, the majority were employed in agriculture. Of those employed (43% were unemployed when caught), 26% were earning less than $1.00 per hour; 56% between $1.00 and $2.00; 14% between $2.00 and $3.00, and 3% were earning over $3.00 per hour. Almost 10% said they belonged to a union. Of those employed, most were sending between one-fourth and three-fourths of their wages to Mexico.

One-fifth admitted to having been in jail in Mexico serving a sentence. Four percent admitted to having been in jail in the U.S.

Most of the aliens were born in a rural area, and only 16% were born in a city. We had the notion that most of the aliens would have been residents of one of the six Mexican border states before their entry into the U.S. This idea came from studying the internal migration patterns in Mexico between 1940 and 1960.

We asked where the alien had lived during the five years before entering the U.S. Fifty percent said they had lived in one of the six border states.

Gamio (1930:13) states that the source of Mexican immigration to the U.S., while distributed throughout Mexico, was in

TABLE 11
STATE OF BIRTH OF 493 WETBACKS
(see map below)

No. on Map	State	Number	Percentage (N = 493)	No. on Map	State	Number	Percentage (N = 493)
1	°Chihuahua	91	18.46	16	Federal District	5	1.01
2	Durango	49	9.94	17	Queretaro	4	.81
3	Michoacán	41	8.32	18	State of México	4	.81
4	Guanajuato	41	8.32	19	Aguascalientes	3	.61
5	Jalisco	37	7.51	20	Veracruz	2	.41
6	San Luis Potosí	36	7.30	21	Colima	1	.20
7	Zacatecas	34	6.90	22	Puebla	1	.20
8	°Nuevo León	30	6.09	23	Chiapas	1	.20
9	°Tamaulipas	25	5.07	24	Yucatan	1	.20
10	°Coahuila	24	4.87	25	Territorio de Baja California	1	.20
11	Sinaloa	13	2.64	26	Oaxaca	0	0
12	°Sonora	12	2.43	27	Tlaxcala	0	0
13	°Baja California	8	1.63	28	Campeche	0	0
14	Nayarit	6	1.22	29	Quintana Roo	0	0
15	Guerrero	6	1.22	30	Morelos	0	0
				31	Hidalgo	0	0
				32	Tabasco	0	0
					No Answer	17	3.45
					Total	493	100.00%

°Border States

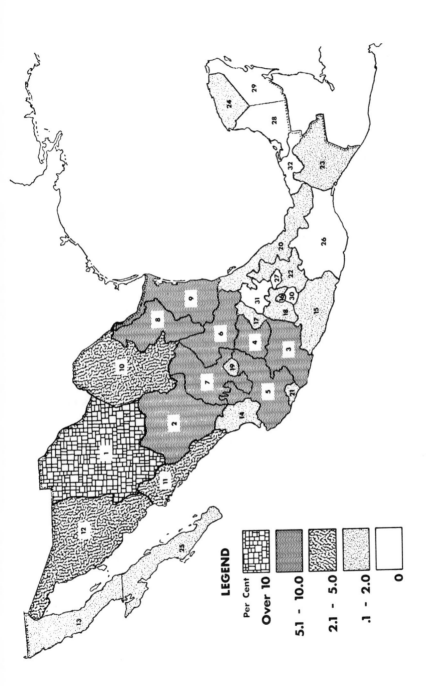

LEGEND

Per Cent

Over 10

5.1 - 10.0

2.1 - 5.0

.1 - 2.0

0

large part from the states of the Central Plateau and in lesser proportion from the Northern Plateau. In his study, he shows that over 60% of the immigrants came from four states (Michoacán, Guanajuato, Jalisco, and Nuevo León), the last one being a border state. The data from Saunders and Leonard (1951:31) reveal that 70% of the wetbacks in their study were born in the above four states plus San Luis Potosí.° Our own research indicates that the above five states were the birthplace of 38% of the aliens interviewed. But if we look at the birthplace of 73% of the aliens, we must include the five states mentioned plus three others (Chihuahua, Durango, and Zacatecas). If we look at the percentage of the aliens born in the six border states (Chihuahua, Nuevo León, Tamaulipas, Coahuila, Baja California, and Sonora), the figure is 38%. Thus, over the years the source of aliens has become more widely distributed throughout Mexico with less concentration in two or three states. And the six border states, following the internal migration patterns, are beginning to supply more and more of the wetbacks as judged by place of birth. See Table 11 and the accompanying map.

To sum up the demographic characteristics of our sample we may say that we are dealing with a young population, mostly males, about half of whom are single. Their educational achievement is very low, their knowledge of English is nil for the very great majority. They are unskilled agricultural workers. Their income is low and their opportunities to obtain employment before being apprehended are limited. Most have been apprehended more than once; some have lived in the U.S. several years and have relatives here, including children, who are U.S. citizens.

Why Do You Play the Game?

The individual in Mexico who finds himself unemployed, without land or capital assets and with a family to support, is considerably limited in the avenues of action open to him in order to stay alive. He may beg or steal; his relatives and friends may help him; he may have to eat garbage. A woman

° The data for Saunders and Leonard was taken from only one detention center, therefore not representing all the possible sources.

may prostitute herself. If the individual lives in the rural area, he may be lured to the city in search of employment. If he has heard of the Bracero Program, of wetbacks and of commuters, and of the exaggerated stories about the wealth of the U.S., the jobs available, the high wages and the ease of crossing the border, he will head north, as do hundreds of thousands of persons. Once in the border area, the next major problem (besides surviving) is to cross the border. Once across the border the problem is to avoid the Border Patrol and to find a job.

It is not difficult to comprehend the poverty-induced desperation which will compel a man to endure whatever hardship and humiliation in order to be able to obtain a few pesos for the sheer survival of his family and himself.

Most wetbacks understand that they will not be successful. But when one is at the bottom of the social heap there is no place or position below you. And then there is always hope. Hope that you can hold on to a job, without official detection, to provide sustenance for the family. Many wetbacks have higher aspirations. Some talk of saving money to buy land back in Mexico. Others hope to establish a small business. Some would buy a car and go into the taxi business. It appears to us that those who have higher aspirations are also those who move farther north seeking industrial jobs. They also seem to be the ones with more experiences, more apprehensions. We suspect, too, that they have more education, are more literate, and can handle English better.

Our interviews in a federal prison near the border revealed that many wetbacks come to the door to be apprehended and put in prison, not realizing that it isn't that easy to be imprisoned. When they learn that they must commit a crime or violate deportation regulations, many will do something in order to be imprisoned, particularly during the winter months. At this prison, which provides medical care, adult education classes, good clothes, warm and comfortable living accommodations and excellent food, a wetback may work in one of several occupations and send a tidy check home to his family. It is theoretically possible, if he stays long enough, to be adequately trained, at government expense, in English, U.S. history and culture, and some vocation so that in the future his survival in the U.S. without apprehension is less problematic.

Wetbacks, by definition, are law violators. They have violated a federal law and are subject to legal deportation. With the establishment of the Border Patrol an administrative procedure was instituted called voluntary departure. Thus if a wetback has no criminal record and has not been deported before, he can be expelled from the U.S. within days of being apprehended.

On one occasion the author saw some two hundred wetbacks at the San Ysidro holding center on the California border. These men had been brought in during the day from various parts of California and were to be sent to El Centro for processing. By the time the author arrived at the detention center in El Centro the following morning at 8:30 A.M., the last busload had been processed and was on its way to Mexico. They had been bussed from San Ysidro at midnight, arrived at El Centro at 4:00 A.M. and processed in four hours. With the illegal traffic what it is, imagine the cost if each man had to be formally deported! If it is correct that over 200,000 Mexican illegals were apprehended in 1969, then an average of 547 aliens must have been processed daily in three detention centers.

A Life of Uncertainty

The wetback who has entered the U.S. is a fugitive from the law. He knows that the Border Patrol is after him and that it has a long arm. To begin with there are tracking specialists who can follow him for miles once his tracks are picked up. These specialists are assisted by pilots in small planes who are in contact with jeeps and cars equipped with radios. He also knows that if he attempts to use the commercial transportation system (bus, train, airplane), the Border Patrol consistently checks the depots and terminals and even the carriers. One of the better ways of escaping detection is to travel by taxi (which is expensive), or for a group to buy or rent an old car.

Once at his destination he is confronted with the problem of settling in. This means that he must find a place to live and a job. The majority of the wetbacks are apprehended on roads and streets and while looking for employment. Thus, even if he has left the border undetected, he is still in danger of apprehension.

Whenever and wherever possible he moves into the "Mexican" section of town. Here relatives, friends, or Mexican-Americans will help, many for a price.

Although we have indicated that the wetback may not consider himself to be living in a completely strange culture when in the U.S. (particularly along the border and some urban areas), still, the farther north he moves the greater the cultural differences. Even though every town and city in the U.S. probably has residents who speak Spanish, consider the problems of finding a house, locating a job, and working among English-speaking people. The buying of food either at stores or restaurants can present difficulties. Everyday behavior (purchasing clothes, laundry services, medical attention, etc.) presents difficulties for the wetback. If we consider other areas of social conduct we find similar problems. Where does he go to church? What does he do for recreation? Who are his friends? In a real sense the wetback lives "half a life"—never a participating part of the community or society (he can't vote, for example); always in a strange culture; seldom integrated into the life of the community; with little opportunity for roots or permanence, for example, marriage and establishing a family; and always living with the fear of being apprehended. Any individual with whom he is in contact can turn him in.

The wetback will avoid any situation which requires identification papers and he will avoid relationships with institutions generally. Buying on credit, cashing checks at banks, attending church, any everyday normal activity is fraught with danger.

Family Consideration

Our own research did not go into any depth concerning the quality of life available to the wetback. By and large he feels that he is treated adequately in the U.S.; only four percent felt that they were treated badly. One must consider, however, the circumstances which brought them to the U.S., the socioeconomic situation, and their aspirations. Much research needs to be done on the effects on the individual, the family, and the community of this periodic migrancy. This situation which compels an individual to leave his home, his family, his community, and his country in search of employment must have profound effects on all concerned.

There is no question that such family disruptions can have

deleterious effects on familial relationships, in spite of the economic gain which might ensue. If a father is away from his family for several months at a time, a normal relationship can hardly be expected. Moreover, the small communities from which the aliens come can also be affected by the loss of large numbers of their young adults for extended periods of time. We suggest that the U.S. demand for labor which involved over four million braceros over a twenty-two year period and over five million wetbacks, while beneficial to both Mexico and the U.S. in economic terms, probably created innumerable sociological problems whose consequences are evident today— Problems such as broken homes; illegal marriages in the U.S.; broken marriages when an alien husband is deported; a disproportionate loss of young males in rural areas, leaving high female ratios and a high male ratio in the resident areas where the migration ends; an extremely high increase of population in border cities; an increase in crime, delinquency, prostitution and other social pathologies in areas of disproportionate population growth and skewed sex ratios. These problems, coupled with the more familiar problems of housing, unemployment, hunger, malnutrition, and stark poverty are awesome to consider.

Economic Exploitation

Justification for the employment of wetbacks is often couched in humanitarian terms. It is often said by U.S. employers that without the jobs which they provide to aliens, the aliens would be unemployed and perhaps starving in Mexico. This is probably true. Some employers do provide housing, medical attention, and even education for the children of wetbacks. And this is true in some instances along the border. Many employers north of the border do not discriminate as to wages. But in a broader perspective and particularly in agriculture and along the border the picture is not so rosy.

In a recent study near El Paso, in the summer of 1969, we were told that the going wage for wetbacks in agriculture in this area varied from $.75 to $1.10 per hour. One woman, a Mexican-American of Fabens, Texas, said this to our interviewers: "We get only $1.10. But we can't complain to the government unless all of us complain together. We'd just be black-balled. There are only 100 farms between Clint and the Hudspeth county line. The farmer knows who you are. When Mexicans come over to work for $1.10 the farmer says to us, 'You work for $1.10 too or you don't work. I can get all the labor I want at $1.10!' So we take it." Our interviewer was also told that many Anglo women in this area hire Mexican women as housekeepers. These maids commute daily from Mexico and are paid approximately $2.00 per day.

An article in the *Chicago Tribune* of Sunday, October 5, 1969, said that the Waukegan police and Lake County sheriff's deputies conducted a series of raids on the county's courthouse and arrested six aliens who were working illegally, and had worked for several months. They were hired by Mr. Bailey the building superintendent, who said "Why shouldn't I hire them. They work hard, cause no trouble, are very dedicated, and work for less."

During one of our group interview sessions held in a detention center with two immigration officials present, we heard the following story from three illegal aliens.

They, along with twelve others, were hired by a farmer and went to work at his farm. After working a week they were surprised that the farmer did not say a word about paying their wages. They did not complain because, they said, they did not want to make the farmer angry since he could then turn them in to the Border Patrol. After ten days they decided to ask the farmer for their money. He reacted to the request by giving them five dollars apiece with the promise that he would pay the rest at the end of the week. Our interviewees explained to us that they did not have any other alternative but to agree to continue working and to wait until the end of the week for their money. At the end of the week, they said, the farmer brought a truck and asked them to get into it, saying that he was going to take them to his other farm nearby, where he would pay them their wages. Upon entering the truck they saw two Border Patrol cars waiting right off the limits of the ranch where they were working. They said they realized immediately that they had been turned in by the farmer. Upon being apprehended the aliens told the Border Patrol officials that the farmer owed them their wages of two weeks and that they were on their way to receive their money. The officials answered that they could not wait, but the men would be allowed to make a complaint against the farmer, once in the detention center. The aliens stated that by this time there was no doubt in their minds that there was an agreement between the Border Patrol officials and the farmer, who was not even interrogated about the farm worker's complaints.

On another occasion an informant told us of a situation similar to the one just related. He told us about a farmer who hired wetbacks for ten to fifteen days, after which he just called the Border Patrol and turned them in without having paid their wages. The next day or so he would pick up another fifteen wetbacks on the road or he would just wait for other wetbacks to come asking for a job. He would again work the aliens for ten to fifteen days and repeat the process of turning them in without paying their wages. This situation was brought to the attention of the officials by a neighbor farmer who called to complain that his neighbor was practicing "unfair competition" by failing to pay the cost of his labor force. Many wetbacks had also complained to the officials about the same farmer. When asked to appear before the officials to answer the complaints, the farmer refused. The complaining farmer also refused to make a statement, saying that he just wanted the Border Patrol to stop his neighbor's practice of not paying the wetbacks' wages, but he did not want to pursue any legal action against his neighbor.

In spite of all efforts made by the Border Patrol officials to control the type of situations reported above, we learned that in Texas once the farmer negates the charges of failure to pay wages the officials' only recourse is to turn the case over to other authorities in charge of the enforcement of the laws related to labor.

We have learned also that in the whole lower Rio Grande valley in Texas there is only one investigator in charge of the enforcement of those laws. We also found that the law that proscribes failure to pay wages on the part of the employer does not prescribe the obligation of the employer to pay the wages owed. Once the employer is found guilty he must pay a fine of fifty dollars regardless of the amount of wages that he failed to pay.

Art. 5157, R.C.S. Penalty for Failure to Pay.

Every person, partnership or corporation, willfully failing or refusing to pay the wages of any employee at the time and in the manner provided in this statute shall forfeit to the State of Texas the sum of fifty dollars for each and every such failure or refusal. Suits for penalties accruing under this law shall be brought in any court having jurisdiction of the amount in the county in which the employee should have been paid, or were employed. Such suits shall be instituted at the direction of the Commissioner of Labor Statistics by the Attorney General or under his direction, or by the county or district attorney for the county or district in which suit is brought. [Acts 1915 quoted in Texas State Bureau of Labor Statistics, 1959:29]

As we look through the literature we find that no less a person than John Nance Garner (former vice-president of the U.S.) was making statements about the need the growers had for the cheapest possible labor in order to make a profit. He was referring to Mexican labor (U.S. Congress, Committee on Immigration and Naturalization, Hearings, 1926:20–23). McWilliams (1949:191) quotes a deputy sheriff before the LaFollette Committee hearings stating that they had to protect the farmers in Kern County because they were the best people and kept the county going. With reference to the Mexican laborers he said, "But the Mexicans are trash. They have no standards for living. We herd them like pigs." Senator McCarran, in 1953, stated that the agricultural people along the border needed the wetbacks because they just couldn't get along without them and that we might just as well face the situation realistically (McCarran, 1953). He was implying that the legislation must reflect realistically the need for cheap labor. Saunders and Leonard (1951), in their study in 1949, documented quite clearly the exploitation of cheap labor in the lower Rio Grande valley. Hadley (1956) has also documented this exploitation of labor, as did Galarza (1964).

We find then a situation in which poor people from a developing nation attempt to make a living in another nation at wages which are low but acceptable from their nation's standard. In order to do this, however, they must violate laws, suffer indignities and many inconveniences. They must live in substandard conditions, away from their families, always in fear of being apprehended and without being integrated into the community or the society in which they may live. In the process they keep wages down, they displace American labor, and they hamper the efforts of the American labor unions to organize and to bargain collectively. On the one hand it is not difficult to understand why unemployed Mexican aliens cross the border, nor why employers are so willing to hire them. This is the readily available labor force. They have absolutely no rights in the host country. They have absolutely nothing to say about the wages which they will receive. They are single individuals for the most part. They are a docile group by the very conditions under which they are here. They represent a tremendous oversupply of labor and thus can be replaced at will. They have absolutely no bargaining position because the mere threat of being turned in to the Border Patrol prevents bargaining. They can be gotten rid of at a moment's notice, or whenever the harvest is over, and sometimes without even being paid if an employer is really unscrupulous.

From Poverty to Greater Poverty

I was born in Zacatecas, I am twenty-five years old, I have a family of four children and went to school up to fifth grade. I was working as a mason in my home town. A friend of mine told me about an individual who could lend me some money to come to the U.S. and who could get a job for me in the U.S. This individual loaned me 300 pesos ($24.00) at 10 percent interest rate monthly. Since I did not have anything to give him as a guarantee for the loan I was told that if I did not pay the money back something would happen to my wife or my children. I did not have any alternative and I accepted that condition. Fifteen days after having crossed the border as a wetback I was caught by the Border Patrol. I had only worked one week, therefore I did not even make enough money to pay the loan, so I went back to see the person who loaned me the money because I did not want anything to happen to my family. I told him that I would pay him back as soon as I could get a job.

After begging him for a while he agreed to loan me 500 pesos more, this time at 15 percent monthly interest. I gave 400 pesos to my wife from the new loan and came back to the border by hitchhiking. I crossed the river again as a wetback. That was a bad time of the year for jobs and I did not find any until a month later. In order to avoid the Border Patrol I did not go to the towns and I slept hidden in the desert every night. From my hideaway I went out to look for jobs in the nearby ranches. The money I made went to pay the interest due. I worked for two months and I was caught while going to the post office to send money to my wife. Now, after I'm returned to Mexico, I will have to ask for more money in order to be able to come back once again. I have to come back to the U.S. because I would never find a job in Mexico which would allow me to make enough money to pay my debts. It is too bad that this time the rate of interest will probably be higher, as will my debt and my problems. [Paraphrased from an interview in a detention center]

Although we have no statistical evidence for the following statement, it is our contention that the illegal traffic in the form of wetbacks from Mexico to the United States has not generally been beneficial to Mexico, to the families of the wetbacks, nor to the wetback himself. The basis for this opinion is the fact that most wetbacks are caught before they find work or while they are seeking employment, and most of them are caught close to the U.S.-Mexico border. (Refer to Chapter V, especially Table 7.)

Our analysis of all the data available to us indicates a breakdown of the illegal traffic into five categories.

The first category is those wetbacks who work regularly, mostly in agriculture, along the border. Many of these workers are employed year after year by the same employers during particular periods, and some of them are accompanied by their families. Some are in a sense commuters, moving daily in and out of Mexico for their agricultural jobs. Some are holders of the visitors and shoppers permit (Form I-186), and these, too, are generally commuters either daily or periodically, some of whom work as maids in the U.S. border towns. We suggest that for this category working in the United States is "profitable" and there is some periodic permanence year in and year out in these occupations. To people in this category being a wetback is beneficial and Mexico is also benefitted by their "stable" employment.

A second category is those who cross the border in search of work but who are apprehended before they are employed. This probably represents the majority of the wetbacks and they probably do not benefit financially from their experiences. When these people return to Mexico they probably are no better off, and perhaps less well off than when they first ventured into the United States.

A third category are those who are smuggled into the United States and are caught within a relatively short time. These people who have paid from $100 to $300 for the opportunity to come to the United States and locate a job are probably those who suffer the most financially because of the investment which they have made and the loan which now has to be paid off.

The fourth category are those who cross the border, either by themselves or through a smuggling operation, and who escape the border and end up in the northern areas of the United States, but who eventually are apprehended. These illegals are likely to be fairly successful, staying in the United States from thirty days to over a year. A look at Table 7 (Chapter V) suggests that several thousand, perhaps close to fifty thousand, have managed to stay in the United States between one month and over a year. If this group has managed to escape the border area and to find employment, they probably have made fairly good wages, particularly in those areas removed from the border.

A fifth category is those who succeed. These are the wetbacks who have eluded the Border Patrol and who have escaped the border region. No one knows how many have been able to do this, and it would even be difficult to venture a guess.

Of the five categories suggested here, categories four and five are probably the most profitable for Mexico, for the wetback families, and the wetback himself, because this means that illegals have managed to work in the United States and to send money back to Mexico. Those in category number one have also managed to provide some kind of a livelihood for their families, which in turn has been beneficial to Mexico. Those in categories two and three have probably found the experience of being a wetback more costly than beneficial.

Since we know nothing of the life ways of category five we can not say much about it. However, in the first four categories even to the extent that the wetbacks have been successful in finding employment and escaping apprehension for this particular period of time, it is still reasonable to assume that the wetback experience has been economically beneficial only up to a point. Many of the persons whom we have interviewed, besides suggesting the economic exploitation that has taken place while they have been employed, have also indicated that upon being apprehended they have lost economically in terms of wages or clothing and goods left behind. Considering the fact that they have had to pay either room and board or rent and maintenance for themselves, considering the fact that many of them have not been here very long, it has been difficult for many to make any kind of savings before being apprehended. Many wetbacks told us also that, upon being returned to Mexico, Mexican officialdom has regularly taken whatever money they had accumulated under the threat that if they did not relinquish their money they would be charged with some misdemeanor or felony such as smuggling of drugs and would be placed in jail.

We suggest then that in the process of playing this game, the illegal, whatever his motivations and his aspirations, probably moves from poverty to greater poverty and, whatever his experiences, the economic and financial benefit for Mexico, for his family, and for himself is small. Those who profit are those who employ him or who smuggle him.

vii: *Through the Eyes of a Wetback — A Personal Experience*

Our concern to cover all possible aspects of the wetback story kept us searching for means and methods of gathering more information and of controlling the reliability and validity of that information already obtained. We decided that the technique of participant observation could be validly used, and a Mexican researcher thoroughly familiar with literature on wetbacks as well as the research project was engaged to become a wetback. The Immigration and Naturalization Service in Washington would be advised of the general plan (but not the details) in order to protect the observer's legal status in the U.S. in the future and in case of unforeseen difficulties relative to his safety. The observer was to leave all of his documentation, together with a letter from the director of the project, in the hands of a lawyer in a U.S. border city. The observer was to go to Mexico, assume the clothing and behavior of a lower-class worker from the interior, and upon reaching a Mexican border city he was to seek assistance in crossing illegally into the U.S. Upon crossing the border he would behave as a wetback along with his companions. He would try to obtain employment, be apprehended by the Border Patrol, sent to a detention center, and expelled from the country. During this period the observer would keep a diary and careful notes of his experience and send the materials to the research project in the form of letters. Below is a summary of his report.

The Participant Observer's Report°

Dressed like the type of wetback I was planning to portray, and with twenty-five dollars in my pocket, I crossed the U.S.-Mexican border at Hidalgo, Texas, and arrived at Reynosa, Tamaulipas, Mexico, where I went to the *plaza principal* and started walking around, looking for persons who were planning to cross the river into the U.S. Previous information was confirmed on the openness with which people speak about crossing the river without the benefit of the bridge.

On this morning I was able to join four groups in the main square who were discussing the details of crossing. I was interested not only in what they were talking about but also, of course, in the way I was received and accepted as any other would-be wetback. In spite of some differences in speech, through which they noticed I was not a peasant, they allowed me in their conversation without any apparent suspicion. The story I had prepared was that I was born and raised in Zamora, Michoacán; my mother was a maid for a wealthy family for whom I was working as a servant (houseboy). I went to school, finishing *secundaria* (junior high school), and four years ago I went to Mexico City to work in construction, where I learned how to operate construction machinery. I was out of a job and that was the first time I was going to cross as a wetback. This story fitted a type which is not uncommon among wetbacks, according to our information, although the urban type of wetback is more likely to cross at El Paso, Texas, or California—where jobs in services may be available—than in the lower Rio Grande valley, where I was. For those who live in the central states of Mexico, this valley is the closest and the least expensive point to reach; it is also the region where the poor peasant is more likely to cross as a wetback.

When a person arrives in a Mexican border town wanting to cross the river illegally for the first time he goes around asking questions on how to do it. Group discussions about crossing without proper documents are so open that a person who arrives in Reynosa in the morning will have found a group the same day and will cross that evening. The one who seems to have the most experience will lead a group of two to

° This chapter was originally written by Jorge A. Bustamante F.

five persons, without any apparent concern about who they are. These groups are frequently approached by smugglers recruiting clients and offering, at varying prices, the safest way to get across the border or beyond the checking points of the Border Patrol. What they offer is not only their knowledge of the terrain but very often contacts for jobs in a great variety of places, from just across the river, to Kansas or the Midwest. Where I was the prices ranged from fifty dollars for being smuggled to the first highway going to McAllen, to $400 for being smuggled to Chicago. Four "coyotes" (smugglers) that I found were green card bearers.

I was looking for a local "veteran wetback" who was planning to cross that day and with whom I could join without having to pay for his assistance. The type I had in mind was one who lives in Reynosa and goes frequently to the U.S. without inspection. So I walked along the river and after several inquiries I found a group of people, all of them residents of El Ejido Longoria, which is located two miles from Reynosa. After I gave them my story, they began to advise me as to how to behave in order to avoid being caught by *la migra* (the Border Patrol). Two men, about forty-five or fifty, were speaking enthusiastically about the bracero epoch during the Second World War. One said, "That was a time when it didn't matter if you were kicked by the gringo because you could make good money." The other added, "After the war everything changed and *echarsela de mojado* [to go as a wetback] *valio madre* [wasn't worth a damn]. The farmers were paying less and less; I think that happened because it seemed like all the Mexicans were crossing the Rio Grande after the war, and particularly during the fifties." Another who seemed to be younger and more educated said, "Where it is worth going nowadays is to Chicago to work in the factories. You make good money. But the problem is the damn weather up there—that cold is not for Christians." A fourth one added, "I am not going anymore because *la migra me la tiene sentenciada* [those of the Border Patrol have a sentence pending on my head] and if they catch me again they will bury me in 'La Tuna' [a federal prison near El Paso] for a long time, and I cannot afford that now."

The owner of the place where we were gathered told me that his nephew was planning to go across that night and he would ask him if I could go along. His nephew, whom we shall call Juan, was twenty-five years old and a "veteran wetback." He was going to San Antonio where he knew someone who could hire him. He accepted my company and everything was settled to leave by sunset. Another "veteran wetback" from the neighborhood came to join us, and although he clearly did not like the idea of going with a first-timer like myself, he finally went with us. We shall call him José.

At 7:30 P.M. Juan respectfully received the blessings of fare-well from his father. His father was bedridden, unable to walk as a result of a tractor accident eight years ago, while working as a bracero near Weslaco, Texas. Juan, his only support, was looking for work in order to buy a long-needed medical pre-scription for his father. He hoped that *this time* he could stay long enough in the U.S. to make the money he needed.

Making the Crossing

We left the house and walked about two miles to the place they knew as the most convenient for crossing. The river was running straight at that place and was about 140 feet wide. They explained that we should not cross where the river curves because, there, deep holes and whirlpools make it dangerous. As we got closer to the crossing point they lowered their voices and tried to walk noiselessly. They warned me about two deeper zones on each side of the river. We were supposed to wade with the exception of the last twenty feet, where we would have to swim. We were to cross diagonally along with the current, carrying our clothes in plastic bags.

Very quietly we took off our clothes and began the crossing. They were ahead of me and I saw them sinking until the water reached two inches from their shoulders. Right then I realized I would have problems, because they were taller than I. I stepped on the bottom of the river, which was muddy on the surface but became firm an inch deeper. The water was soon over my shoulders and I could no longer stand against the stream. Juan realized my problem and told me to throw my bag to him so that I could swim freely. I drifted about twelve feet downstream from them; perhaps this was why each time I tried to touch the bottom I could not, yet I saw that they were still walking. I should mention that I have always had trouble swimming for a distance longer than a hundred feet, so in the middle of the river I began to feel tired. At this point I tried for the last time to touch the ground in order to rest. I had seen them in the middle of the river, with the water at their waist, but I was unable to keep my vertical position because where I was crossing the river was deeper. I decided not to try walking again and kept on swimming for the rest of the crossing. There was a point when I thought that I couldn't make it; I was exhausted. I heard Juan asking if I needed help. I did not answer but made the last effort to reach the U.S. edge of the river.

It took me a while to recover enough to try to climb the bank, which, at that point, was slanted more than forty degrees. I couldn't do it, so, holding onto the grass at the river's edge, I pulled myself along to the point where Juan and José were waiting for me. When I finally did reach them they were staring at me in a way that seemed to indicate I was doing things wrong. Later they explained that they had chosen that point of the river for crossing because we could wade most of the way. They said that one should stay immersed as much as possible because a naked person wading the river is very difficult to see at night but a person swimming becomes very easy to spot if he splashes while swimming. The splashing noise I made while swimming and trying to climb the bank made them fear that we might have been seen by the Border Patrol. José said, "When I saw you swimming with that *chapoteadero* [splashing], it seemed like you were making signs to call *la migra*." It was clear that I had done all the things they were trying not to do.

Once I finally stood up on the river bank, Juan motioned to me to be quiet and hide myself in the grass. We were there for more than twenty minutes just waiting, alert to any noise that would indicate that the Border Patrol had spotted us. We stayed naked so that we could cross back quickly should they approach. There was a moment, while we were waiting, when Juan and José said a prayer very quietly, just moving their lips, with their arms crossed and serious expressions on their faces.

Evading the Patrol

It was already dark, but not totally dark. The clouds did not hide the moon as Juan had anticipated. This disturbed them a little—to the extent of causing them to swear at the uncooperative wind. Finally, Juan climbed up to the top of the bank, where a dirt road went along the U.S. side of the river. He watched for a while and then came down, telling us to get dressed quickly. The plan was to move away from the river as fast as possible. Walking on the road was very dangerous, for the Border Patrol might come at any moment, and it would be easy to see a person walking across the newly planted fields. We crossed the road and decided to crawl through the fields. This distance was long and difficult for me to cover. José and Juan crawled faster than I, with almost feline movements that contrasted with the difficulties I found in crawling while carrying the bag that held my clothes and a bottle of water. After the first three fields planted with peppers, we continued through several cotton fields, which provided better hiding and made it unnecessary to crawl. We did not stop for approximately two miles until we got to a dirt road. We were crossing a third dirt road when the lights of a car appeared. We immediately ran into the bushes to hide, lying down. After the car passed by they urged me to move faster whenever the lights of a car approached. At that hour of the night we must assume that any car would be a Border Patrol car. The next time we saw the lights of a car I did exactly what they told me, but a tremendous noise made clear again who was the novice; my water bottle fell and broke. Once again I saw a couple of serious faces as we came out of our hiding places. Shaking his head, José made the only comment, "We were again very lucky that it wasn't a Border Patrol car. The noise you made was heard in McAllen." I just said, "I am sorry."

We were approaching McAllen, but we did not plan to enter the city but rather to go around it toward Edinburg, Texas. We crossed Highway 83, which is west of McAllen, and continued through orange fields, when a dog began barking. We then changed direction, and Juan said, "This is too bad, that dog was barking at people." I asked him what he meant and he said, "Don't you know that dogs bark differently depending upon what they are barking at? Now the people in the house know by the barking that we are here. They might have called the police, so let's get out of here quickly. If the town police catch us it will be worse for us than if we were caught be the Border Patrol. Those *chotas* [cops] are really bad with Mexicans." We ran from that field and didn't stop until we had crossed another highway going northeast toward Edinburg.

Our First Encounter

We were crossing a farm road when Juan asked José to hold his bag while he took a stone from his shoe. He was almost through when we heard a car coming. This time I ran faster than they and got deeper in the thicket. I felt Juan behind me and I saw José stoop to pick up the things he was carrying, thus losing a few seconds. The car was making a turn when its headlights spotted us just before we had hidden ourselves. I heard the car stop and its door open, then a loud voice saying, in Spanish, "Come out immediately. We have seen you." No one moved and I decided to wait and see what Juan and José would do. The same voice repeated, "Don't play games with us because it will be worse for you. You'd better come up or we will go and get you."

Again no one made any noise, but we could hear the officers walking on the road. Then a second voice said, "Let's go and get them," and the other answered, "No, wait."

Then again the first voice said, "Don't make us angry, you bastards. Come out right now or I'll make you come out with bullets."

After twenty or thirty seconds I heard three shots.* Ten seconds later the grass moved and one of the officers said, "Here is one." Then, in an angry tone, "Don't get smart—move. Didn't you hear what I said?"

I knew by the distance of the voice that it had been José who had been discovered. There was the sound of a person standing up from the grass, and one of the officers said, "Where are the others?"

José answered quietly, "What others? I am alone."

Then, with the sound of a blow against a body, one officer said furiously, "Do you think we are stupid or blind? We saw all of you and you better tell me where they are."

José said, "They must be far away by now."

* James F. Greene, Associate Commissioner, U.S. Department of Justice, told us "it is definitely against Service policy to strike an alien or to use firearms except in self-defense or in defense of a third party," and he believes this case was an isolated incident.

The other officer told him to get in the car and shouted, "For the last time . . . come out right away or I'll shoot you."

He then shot three times and nothing was heard after that until the other officer said loudly so that we would hear: "Let them go and let the rattlesnakes get them. It's going to be worse for them with the rattlesnakes than with us."

The mention of the snakes scared me more than the shooting but I didn't move, waiting to see what Juan would do. For some reason the officers never got to our hiding place. I heard voices speaking in English and then the car left. I stayed quiet for maybe four or five minutes more, waiting for Juan to make the first move. I had the sensation that I was surrounded by rattlesnakes and that at any moment I would feel one biting me. It also came to my mind that since Juan was not moving, perhaps one of the shots had killed him. Finally Juan got up and went to the road to look. I saw his silhouette coming back. He began to laugh nervously, and then louder and louder, hysterically. I shook him to make him stop. Once calmed down he said, "This is a miracle of the Virgin of Perpetuo Socorro . . . she made them leave without having them come to look for us. They never do that, they never leave when they have spotted a wetback." Then he said, "We must get out of here. They might come back now that they know we are around."

We continued walking toward Edinburg, not without regretting what had happened to José. Juan said, "Poor guy, I think he will be taken now to 'La Tuna' for sure. He has been on probation. Well, that's the way it is in this business. He wanted to make money to buy a bicycle in order to be eligible for a job as a bill collector in Reynosa. Now he won't need money for a while."

Juan anticipated a new search by the Border Patrol and we had to move fast. He asked me for a road map of Hidalgo County which I had told him a cousin of mine had given to me when he knew that I was going to come to the border. By the light of a match we looked at the map and Juan located ourselves northeast of McAllen, near Twenty-third Street which goes north. He guessed that the Border Patrol would look for us thinking that we would follow Twenty-third Street or a drainage ditch to Edinburg. Juan decided to take neither of these logical alternatives but to go east and stop at some point near Tenth Street, where we would sleep until there was

Official U.S. Border Patrol photo

Tracks are easily spotted in sandhills like these near El Paso, where the boundary leaves the Rio Grande and proceeds west overland. The area is patrolled with jeeps and light airplanes.

The Patrol checks farms in the border area in search of aliens who have entered the U.S. illegally or who are working without a permit.

Amalgamated Meat Cutters

Tales of Yankee affluence have attracted many across the border. What they find is a life of hardship, and the most primitive accommodations are not unusual.

Texas Labor Archives photos

First stop for the apprehended illegal alien is often a local jail. From there he is sent to a detention center for processing.

One of three aliens discovered under a truck van in California.

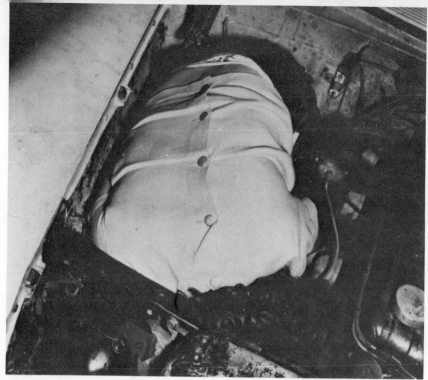

Official U.S. Border Patrol photo

In one of the more daring methods of entry, a young woman was found huddled next to the automobile engine. The man in the bottom photo tried an equally uncomfortable and risky space beneath the hood.

Official U.S. Border Patrol photo

enough traffic to hitchhike to Starr County. We would not enter Edinburg but turn north, taking Jackson Road to Monte Cristo Road. When we arrived at a place where we could get food and water, we would decide whether to continue toward Lake Edinburg.

Our next problem was the lack of water. I had broken my bottle and José had been caught with Juan's bag and his bottle of water. Very soon our thirst became our main concern and we changed directions toward a place where Juan knew there was a pond used for irrigation. I was impressed with Juan's knowledge of the terrain. It was very dark but he was walking with apparent certainty, checking our location with signs that he had anticipated. Finally we arrived at the pond. We had to hang down from the side of the pond, without being able to see the level of the water because of the darkness. It had a very stagnant smell, but at that moment I couldn't have cared less. Since we had no way to carry water, we wouldn't be able to drink again for eight to ten hours.

An hour and a half later we reached Tenth Street and Juan found a spot where the grass was high enough to provide a good hiding place for us to sleep. I was extremely tired, but I had not forgotten the officer's threat about the rattlesnakes. Juan did not sound very convincing to me when he said, "Don't worry, *hombre*, remember that we had a sign already that the Virgin is taking care of us. She will keep the snakes away from us." The advantage of Juan's great faith was evident two minutes later when Juan was snoring and I was awake waiting to be bitten.

The next morning Juan awakened me, saying that it was past eight o'clock and we must continue. We hitchhiked from that point to the crossing of Sugar Road and SH 107, which is closer to Edinburg than the point that Juan had in mind the day before. Juan said he knew a place where we could find a job for the day, but I was not in any physical condition to work. I told him to go ahead without me and that I would go into Edinburg to look for some medicine for my feet. The long walk of the night before had been too much for my feet, which were accustomed to being beneath a desk. Dark stains of coagulated blood were showing over the broken leather of my shoes and I feared an infection. Juan did not want to go into the town, so we decided to meet at the same place between five and six o'clock that evening.

I went into Edinburg and spent the day taking care of my feet and writing notes. While in Edinburg I spoke English all the time in order to lessen the possibilities of being turned in to the Border Patrol. I went to a hotel and rented a room for two dollars, then to a pharmacy and to the public library. About four o'clock I had finished my notes and sent the original copy to Mexico City and one to South Bend, Indiana.

Late in the afternoon I went to the place where Juan and I were to meet, but he did not show up. I returned to Edinburg quite confused about how to carry out my plans. I realized how much I was depending upon him for what I was doing. I thought I wouldn't be able to continue north without somebody's guidance and I was not in good enough physical condition to continue walking; so I went to the bus station in Edinburg, where I thought I could find an Immigration official who would apprehend me. I opened the door and the first person I saw was an officer checking the documents of another man. He was looking at an I.D. against the light and stared at me for a second as I was entering. I thought he was going to stop me but he continued what he was doing, and finally I heard him say that the document was false and he would take the individual to the Border Patrol station. The official then took the man by the arm and walked out, passing very close to where I was sitting.

I left the place five minutes later with the idea of sending a note to my lawyer telling him about my plans. Two blocks from the bus station I heard "psst . . . psst." Turning, I saw Juan hidden in a thicket of a vacant lot. He made a sign with his hand asking me to come close, and it took me two minutes to express to him how happy I was to see him again. He told me he couldn't make it at our appointed time because he was delayed arguing with the foreman where he had worked all day. The foreman refused to pay him as he had promised to do at the end of the day. He said that Juan must stay until the weekend. Juan insisted on the terms he had made when he was hired, but he had to run away after the foreman threatened to call the Border Patrol. I was moved by the fact that Juan was looking for me in Edinburg in spite of his determination not to enter any town until after passing the immigration checking points further north of the border.

I convinced him to accompany me to a hotel instead of sleeping outside as we had the night before. Very reluctantly he accepted and we went to the same hotel where I had been earlier. The next morning we had breakfast and bought some cans of food and juices for our journey.

Under Juan's assumption that the checking point was located approximately ten miles south of Falfurrias, Texas, on U.S. 281, we planned to hitchhike and get off before that point. Then we would walk north through the countryside east of the highway, skipping the checking point and going back to the highway near Falfurrias, where we should arrive before dark.

This time it took us longer to get a ride; traffic was heavy but the cars did not stop. We were finally picked up by a person who looked Mexican and who spoke to us in Spanish. His first question was, "Are you wetbacks?" Juan and I answered at the same time. He said "no" and I said "yes." The driver smiled and told us that it did not matter to him. He said that the Border Patrol had moved north two days ago, so we could get off further north than the point we had told him, but Juan insisted that we get off where he had planned. He then told me, "That guy was very suspicious. I think he wanted to turn us in to the Border Patrol himself." I said that my impression had been the opposite and that it seemed to me he was trying to help us. Juan then said, "You will learn very soon that you cannot trust a person who wears a tie; rich people hate us in this country even if they are of our race." I thought that was a very interesting definition of the situation.

An Episode of Snakes

It was perhaps 10:30 when we jumped over a fence which ran along the highway. We passed the first three hours without incident to speak of. Juan was leading with the same apparent self-confidence that he had shown previously. He was walking ahead of me and we were going up a little hill when Juan suddenly stopped and raised his arm in order to make me stop behind him. I asked him what happened, but a noise, one that I had been fearing to hear since the night

when Jose was caught, gave me the answer. I thought I was
seeing the longest rattlesnake I had ever seen, but it turned
out to be two snakes together. Juan just said, "You see why
we should not walk through here by night?" We went around
the snakes and Juan said, as though talking to himself, "Yes,
I think those bodies we found were of guys who were bitten
by snakes." I was shaken by the comment and by the way he
was taking the fact of having found two bodies earlier in the
year on the same route we were following.

I asked him how he had found those corpses. He said that
he was walking with two others approximately two miles north
of where we were when they found a corpse with part of the
skeleton showing, which made them believe that he had died
perhaps a month before. The corpse still had some clothes on,
but they couldn't ascertain either his age or any physical
features for identification. They made a cross and put it over
him. Later in the same day they found another body. This one
apparently had died more recently, judging from the state of
the clothes. Juan found a letter in one of his pockets, but the
writing was almost totally erased. He took the letter with him
with the idea of looking at it more carefully later on to see if
he could find any clue to his name or the name of a relative
whom he could notify. Juan was thinking of doing this because
he was very much concerned about the soul of the person they
found dead. He said, "If no one knows that guy died, no one
is praying for his soul. And if no one is praying for him, his
soul will be wandering around suffering."*

I insisted on knowing more details about those encounters
but Juan said, "What's the matter with you? What more can
one tell about death? They were dead, that's all . . . everybody
takes that chance in this business and when the time comes for
you you've got what God's will has determined and that's all."
I think he meant that finding a person dead in that area should
be considered normal or expected. Juan's calm while speaking
about the two bodies was impressive. He laconically summarized what he meant by saying, "They just didn't make it."
Obviously, I couldn't see the situation from that perspective.
I was shocked. I felt a profound sadness that immediately

---

* Juan was never able to identify the body because he was apprehended
and the letter seized by the Border Patrol.

evolved into a bitter feeling of frustration. For me those bodies represented cases of murder: two human beings killed by a social system, by creating and maintaining the circumstances in which people find death while looking for the scarce avenues to escape from misery, a misery for which the social system where they lived or died is responsible.

Juan spoke about the bodies with a mixture of sadness and fatalism, shaking his head slowly while looking at the ground and distractedly hitting one of his shoes with a twig. He made me think that if we hadn't had that encounter with the rattlesnakes he wouldn't have told me about something that for him was not unusual enough to be mentioned.

Our Second Encounter

We had been walking for more than four hours and were going up a little hill from the top of which Juan wanted to check our location when we saw a jeep coming in our direction. It appeared so suddenly that we did not have time to hide ourselves. We stood still, looking at the jeep, which stopped about sixty feet from us. Three people got out and pointed their rifles at us. Our reaction was to get down on the ground; then they began to shoot. After the first shots it was obvious that they did not want to kill us but they kept on shooting and all the while we could hear them laughing and shouting. One of the bullets must have hit very close to me because I felt little pieces of dirt hitting my head.

They stopped shooting and came to us, laughing and insulting us in English. One of them told Juan something like, "Get up, you greaser, you are not dead."

We stood up and one of them asked me in very broken Spanish if I knew what "No Trespassing" meant; I said I did not. Then he said in English something like "You damn Mexicans don't know anything about law . . . you only know how to steal, huh?"

Then another said in an angry tone, "You better tell all the 'wets' to stop coming through this ranch." He added in broken Spanish that the next time they would shoot at us to kill.

Then a third one went to the jeep and talked to somebody by radio, stating that they had caught two "wets" and they were going to turn us in to the Border Patrol. Meanwhile the other two tied our hands behind our backs and told us to get in the jeep.

On the way to the checking point of the Border Patrol, they were making jokes about how scared we looked, and one of them asked the driver what would have happened if, *by accident*, they killed us. The driver said that an accident is an accident and nobody would say anything if you killed somebody who has trespassed on your private property, particularly if he is an outlaw, as in the case of all "wets." Before we reached the Border Patrol they untied our hands. The driver told one of the Patrol officers that they worked on a ranch and had found us "very probably" looking for a cow to kill. He added, "Last week we found a cow being killed by them . . . . You know how they are," he said. "They come starving from Mexico and we are the ones who pay for it."

The officer asked him how many wetbacks were working on the ranch. The one who was driving the jeep answered, "Gee, I don't know. How can you tell who is 'wet' and who isn't? We tell the people we hire that we don't want 'wets,' but it's impossible to know who is lying and who isn't."

The officer asked me if they had done anything to us. I showed my wrists, which were red from having been tied behind my back. The Patrolman looked accusingly at the driver of the jeep, who said, "He was trying to escape."

The Patrolman asked Juan to show his wrists, which were also red, and turning to the driver asked, "Was he trying to escape also?"

I was encouraged by what seemed to be a non-supporting reaction from the Border Patrol officer to what the jeep driver had said. I confirmed this suspicion when we were taken inside the station wagon, where the Border Patrol had a mobile office equipped with air conditioning, radio, and office equipment. They had asked Juan how we were caught and he just said, "Shooting at us with their rifles." While the officials were preparing the papers and forms for interrogating us they were making comments in English—assuming, I suppose, that we didn't understand it—such as, "The problem with those guys is that they watch T.V. too much. They don't know who is 'wet' unless they are hunting them." One of the officers suggested that they report the treatment we received from the ranch guards. The other officer said, "You won't get anything done by that; you know who owns that ranch."

Their comments about the ranch guards made me believe that Juan and I had improved our situation by being in the hands of the Border Patrol.

Although being apprehended was an alternative plan that I had anticipated, once actually detained I felt depressed and frustrated. Juan had shown me a special kind of solidarity that at that moment was present in my mind, together with all of the reasons why he had to cross the border, repeatedly, as a wetback; besides, my role as participant observer did not make me any less humiliated at being surrounded by symbols of authority whose meaning seemed to suggest that we were criminals.

I was first to be interrogated. One of the officials asked me to take out everything from my pockets and my bag. The map I was carrying drew their attention and I was asked where and how I had gotten it. I gave them the same story I had given Juan, that a cousin of mine had taken the map with him to Mexico City, where he gave it to me. Then they asked me questions such as: What is your name? Where do you come from? How old are you? Marital status? Place of birth and date? How many times have you come to the U.S.? How many times have you been caught by Immigration officials? Where did you cross? When and at what time? How many persons crossed with you? Where were you going? What kind of job were you looking for? Who were you going to meet in San Antonio? What is your address in Mexico?

While I was being interrogated by one official the other was watching the cars, which have to make a stop in front of the Border Patrol station wagon and wait until they are motioned through. Sometimes the official got out of the station wagon and went to check the passenger's documents. I noticed they were particularly careful in the control of buses, less careful with trucks, and even less careful with passenger cars. In the half hour I was there they stopped four cars. In every case, the cars stopped were occupied by passengers who were apparently Mexicans or of Mexican ancestry and in all four cases the cars were older models.

Once my interrogation was over the official transmitted all the information by radio. Then he took his turn at watching the cars while the other interrogated Juan and transmitted his information also. They were called twice for reports on cars suspected of being used by smugglers and to inform them that I had no past record, but that Juan was an "old friend of ours," who should be taken to McAllen. From there he would be taken by plane to El Paso. I knew that probably meant that Juan was on his way to meet José in the federal prison of "La Tuna" near El Paso. That was the end of my journey with Juan. His companionship had left an indelible imprint on my mind.

Jail and Detention

What follows from here on was a different kind of depressing experience. I was taken to a jail in Falfurrias, Texas, where I spent almost two days in solitary confinement. Being alone I had some time to reflect on the meaning of what I was doing. It became clear to me how different the meaning of the same situation might be for the persons involved in the "wetback game." There is hardly another situation where symbols of subjection are more evident than inside a jail. Here is where the label of "outsider" that society reserves to some deviants is physically felt upon the so-labeled. Yet, the wetback seems not to consider himself a criminal. I was able to confirm this impression later on in the detention center located near Port Isabel, Texas, where I was taken from the Falfurrias jail. The wetback seems to think of jail as part of his destiny of being poor. One is in jail not because one is immoral or a "bad guy" but because one is poor.

When I was taken from the jail to Port Isabel, we made a stop in the holding station at McAllen to change buses and to be checked again by an official. While this processing was taking place we were in a small room waiting for our name to be called. I felt two eyes staring at me and soon recognized the face. It was the official who saw me at the bus station in Edinburg while he was apprehending another. I tried to look unperturbed, but I saw him asking for my record, pointing at me. He took a look at my report and then he called me and said, "You are not a first-timer. You had a *tarjeta* (Form I-186)* and showed it to me. Now, where is that card?" I told

---

* Form I-186 is the visitor's card which permits entrance into the U.S. for seventy-two hours.

him that he was making a mistake, maybe because he had seen me at the bus terminal but that he never stopped me or asked if I had proper papers. He then seemed to doubt but did not relinquish his impression totally. He asked another official to make a "double check" of my record.

Around 9:00 P.M. we arrived at Los Fresnos, near Port Isabel, Texas. This is where the Border Patrol academy and the detention center are. I had visited the institution twice previously in order to conduct interviews with immigration officials and wetbacks, but this time I was being *taken* inside. I feared someone might recognize me, or even worse, consider my face familiar and conclude from that that I was not a first-timer. Fortunately nothing of this sort happened.

After a light meal in the dining hall we were classified either as Deportees (repeaters) or as "V.R." (Voluntary Return); I was classified in the latter category. They took a fingerprint of our right index finger, which was the first and only personal datum they kept that might lead to my actual identification.

Two officials made a careful check of our personal belongings and asked us to take off all our clothes and shoes for the same purpose. Then all the money and personal belongings were taken away from us, and we received a receipt. I will jump ahead a little to say that there were no complaints on this matter when we got our things back, at least not in the group of 40 with whom I was sent back to Mexico two days later.

The population of the detention center was approximately 250 when I was there. Twenty of the 250 were not Mexicans. They were also being detained for having entered the United States illegally. Fifteen were Chileans, one Spanish, one Lebanese, two from Central America, and one from Jamaica. This group was called by both the officials and the rest of the detainees as *los extranjeros* (the foreigners). Obviously all detainees are actually foreigners but because of the overwhelming ratio of Mexicans that distinction made by the Mexican detainees was also adopted by the officials. The foreigners were the ones called first for meals, which they took separate from the rest. It surprised me to hear from a detainee working in the kitchen that "the foreigners" received more and better food than the rest of the detainees. The explanation for this was that several months ago they had protested the quality and quantity of the food. They have to spend more time in custody because of the red tape involved in their deportation.

The case of the Mexicans has been made by far more expeditious. The foreigner might spend several months in the institution, whereas the Mexican may spend from three days to two weeks, depending upon the circumstances. Since his stay in the center is brief, the Mexican detainee is apparently less resentful of the bad quality of food and he also has less time to take any type of organized action while in custody.

Observations Among Fellow Detainees

I concentrated all my attention on gathering information during my stay in the center. Of all the places where I have tried to collect information on the wetback phenomenon, the detention center has been the most profitable for seeing all kinds of details and aspects related to the wetback's life, and here one learns most about how it feels to be a wetback and why they act the way they do. This is so for several reasons: First, the number of wetbacks gives a wide variety of personal experience. Second, here one wetback speaks to another openly and candidly about his personal experiences because he does not fear further consequences, since he is already detained and on his way back to Mexico. Third, there is so much opportunity for getting together in small groups and talking about whatever one wants. And fourth, the shared ethnic and social background and the fact of being detained itself are conducive to socializing. Since I was taken for a wetback by those around me, I was able to ask questions freely regarding our research interests. My inquiry concentrated on aspects of our research where information was scarce or not clear. The following points were the most relevant to our study.

1. Six detainees said they found corpses on their way north from the border. Particularly interesting was the account of two of them who were caught while finishing the "Christian burial" of a body which appeared to have been dead only a few days. One person told me that his life was saved by three others who found him unconscious as a consequence of not having eaten for three days. Not only did he receive food from them but he was actually carried by them for two days until he recovered strength enough to continue walking by himself. Another three spoke of having found a body whose description and location coincided with one of the bodies which Juan had

talked about. Another told me that on two different occasions he found human skeletons in the desert north of El Paso, Texas. Another spoke of different experiences with rattlesnakes. Some of their stories were very funny, others dramatic. One group encountered twenty rattlesnakes in two days. Two detainees who were caught while being smuggled in a car told me that they had chosen to come "via smuggler" because they would never again try to cross on foot. One of them said, "There are so many snakes that it is crazy to come on foot."

2. In spite of the mechanization of agricultural activities that has been going on in the lower Rio Grande valley, there is still a great demand for labor, which attracts many wetbacks.

3. Out of the group of approximately 100 that arrived with me, only four did not bring any money from Mexico. Approximately half of the group said they found jobs before being apprehended. Of the other half, or those who were apprehended without having found a job, thirty said they spent all the money they brought from Mexico by the time they were caught. This seems to indicate that for approximately half of that group who brought money from Mexico, becoming a wetback made them poorer than they were before. If this is true, one could hypothesize that this is a significant drain on the Mexican economy. The term "significant drain" becomes meaningful when it is considered that 201,636 were apprehended in 1969.

4. With two exceptions all of those who came from the Central Plateau states in Mexico said they chose the Tamaulipas-Texas border to cross because it is the cheapest way to the U.S. from central Mexico.

5. In terms of place of residence in Mexico, the most numerous group was very clearly the one from San Luis Potosí. This fact made me decide to stay in San Luis Potosí for ten days after being expelled from the U.S.

6. From a systematic inquiry with my fellow detainees I deduced the following pattern of behavior: If the wetback is apprehended for the first time it is almost certain that he will cross the border illegally again; if he is apprehended for the second time he will cross illegally again but he will try to cross at a different place on the border. If he is apprehended for the third time he has learned that it is very likely that he will go to court and get a sentence, which is usually suspended. After

this it is probable that he will not cross the border illegally again until the term of his suspended sentence has passed, since he knows that he might have to spend a few months in jail if he is apprehended while his sentence is pending. Once the time of the suspended sentence has passed, he may try crossing illegally again; however, this possibility seems to be diminished by the fact that he knows he might not be granted another suspended sentence.

This seems to indicate that there is a limit to the number of times that a person will take the risk of crossing illegally. Juan and José were exceptions, perhaps because of the fact that they live a few yards from the Rio Grande.

7. There seemed to be a consensus* about the following "principle": the greater the amount of money the intended wetback has, the lesser the possibilities of his being apprehended. With enough money he can either pay a smuggler, buy documents in the black market, wait in a Mexican border town until he can obtain a crossing card from the U.S. Immigration authorities (this card, I-186, will allow him to cross legally but not to work in the U.S.), or get his passport and U.S. tourist visa with which he can enter the U.S. at any point. The tourist visa will have the same restrictions as the Form I-186, the difference being that with the latter he can only go no further than twenty-five miles north of the border and can stay no longer than two days, whereas with the tourist visa he can go to Chicago or Detroit, for example.

8. I spoke with eight detainees who complained that they were not paid by their employers, but instead were turned in to the Border Patrol in order to avoid the payment. Three of those eight told me that an official had called their employers and they had come to the center to pay the wages due. One of the other five told me that their pictures had been taken for identification and that the same official had promised to do his best to get their money, in which case he would send it to them in Mexico. There seemed to be a general opinion that the officers of the detention center try to help those who did not receive their wages.

---

* Consensus was indicated both in spontaneous comments and in answer to questions. For a discussion on participant observation see Becker, 1958:652–660.

On the third day of my stay at the center I was taken with a group of forty to Matamoros, Mexico. We were then switched to a Mexican bus line and were told that no one could get off until we arrived at the city of San Luis Potosí. That was a nine-hour non-stop drive. Once in San Luis Potosí I went to the northeast part of the state, where I stayed for ten days gathering information on how a man decides to become a wetback and on how the stability of the family and the community is affected by this outward migration.

In contacts with wetbacks I had many occasions to witness events and circumstances in which ingenuity, human solidarity, and a sense of loyalty to friends were movingly demonstrated. That was the most rewarding part of my experiences. On the other hand, being exposed to the "meaning configurations" (cf. Schutz, 1967:76) of the wetback life stream increased my awareness that the individual and society should have a greater sense of responsibility for the perpetuation of a social system that has created, or allowed, or maintained the role of the wetback, who is placed in a position where he endangers his physical well-being, his human dignity, and even his life for a pittance.

viii: Unanswered Questions

Cheap Labor

In a recent paper (Samora and Bustamante, 1970) we argue that the insatiable demand for cheap labor in the United States and the rather effective exclusion of immigrants from Asia and southern Europe, by the turn of the century, left Mexico as the chief source of cheap labor for the agricultural and industrial development of the West. As pointed out in the present study, the open border between Mexico and the United States, the commuter situation, the Bracero Program which began as a war emergency procedure and lasted twenty-two years, and the wetback traffic all supply and have supplied the demand for cheap labor in the United States. The consequences of an abundant supply of labor are felt along the border in a number of ways.

One consequence of this massive movement of people has been that wages have either been lowered or they have remained relatively low compared with other parts of the nation. Occupation by occupation, wages are generally lower in the border area than they are in other parts of the country. And even within the same occupation aliens are often paid less than the citizen worker.

If wages are low and even depressed in this area, another consequence appears to be the displacement of citizen labor. This domestic labor, largely unskilled and mostly Mexican-American, has had three choices open to them. (1) to work for the same wages that are being offered, (2) to join the welfare roles if wages are insufficient or work is not available to them, or (3) to leave the area and seek work elsewhere. The third alternative has been chosen by a great many Mexican-Americans, most of whom have joined the agricultural migrant streams out of Texas and to the western, northern and eastern parts of the United States. To justify the hiring of Mexican aliens, employers quite often say that the domestic labor will not work in agriculture. Yet this very same domestic labor does work in agriculture in Indiana, Michigan, North Dakota, Minnesota, California, and elsewhere, but for reasonable wages. The effect of this displacement can be seen in the Midwest and the Great Lakes area, where we are beginning to get concentrations of Mexican-Americans. (See Choldin and Trout, 1969.)

A third consequence has been that related to the unionization and collective bargaining. U.S. labor for years has opposed the Bracero Program, the commuter program, and the employment of aliens generally. Their stance has been that aliens depress wages, displace domestic labor, and prevent effective unionization. If this alien labor is essentially voiceless and temporary and subject to the whims of the employer, then it is not subject to organization and unionization. In many instances alien labor, either legal or illegal, has been used to break strikes. As early as the 1920's, the first Mexicans to be brought to East Chicago, Indiana, in any large numbers were brought there as strikebreakers. As late as 1970, the National Farm Workers Organization charged that their strike against the grape growers in California was effectively stymied by the importation and use of Mexican alien workers.

A fourth consequence of the hiring of cheap alien labor has been that of pitting Mexican-Americans against Mexicans. Since Mexican-Americans have been the chief source of unskilled labor in the border area, they, then, are the ones who are most greatly hurt by the importation of alien labor. They are placed in the intolerable situation of on the one hand helping a fellow "Mexican," who may in fact be a friend or a relative and certainly an ethnic brother, and on the other hand they see that the very presence of the alien affects their wages, their employment, and their relationships with employers. They also clearly see that neither they nor the aliens profit from this situation but that the employer always does.

Mexico's Economic Growth and Internal Migration

Mexico as a developing nation has generally been dependent upon foreign capital for its development. The United States has been the foreign country most highly involved in Mexican economic activities. Although in recent years the trend has been toward less dependence on American capital, Mexico is still greatly dependent on the U.S. as a source of capital, as a market for her exports, and as a source of its highly lucrative tourist trade.

In the past few years Mexico's industrial development has been most impressive. Between 1945 and 1960, for example, electrical output increased 300%, petroleum refining 444%, construction 300%, and manufacturing 218% (Rhodes, 1969: 24). Its increase in gross national product has been equally impressive during this period. As a developing nation under a capitalistic system, Mexico suffers from an unequal distribution of its wealth in that a very small percentage of its citizens own and control most of the wealth (not unlike the United States) and that wealth that is not controlled by the private sector or by the Mexican government is controlled by foreign investors, primarily from the United States. This has led Rhodes (1969:25) to conclude that foreign investment presents obvious dangers to Mexico in that decisions regarding Mexico's economic future tend to be beyond its control and that foreign capital is no longer a constructive force because the outflow of profits has become greater than the inflow of invested capital.

As we have indicated before, Mexico's economic development has been impressive if not phenomenal during the last thirty years, not only in the development of industry but also in the building of houses, the increase in employment opportunities, the building of schools, and in the development of health and medical services with a consequent drop in mortality rates. In spite of all of these developments, however, Mexico's population growth is such that she has been unable to provide for a rapidly increasing population, so that the gap between the rich and the poor remains enormous. While the percentage of people in poverty is decreasing, as is the percentage of people who are illiterate, the actual number of poor and illiterate and unemployed is increasing rapidly.

As Rhodes suggests, 1.8% of Mexico's families received

15.5% of its income in 1963, and only 23% of Mexico's families had monthly incomes of more than 1,000 pesos ($80), and 26% received 300 pesos ($24) or less monthly (1969:25–26). Thus, most of the population does not have enough purchasing power for the marketable products of an industrialized society.

It seems, then, that one should distinguish between an economic growth which favors a small percentage of the population, and in this case also foreign investors, and economic development which provides employment and adequate wages to a large proportion of the population, together with the necessities of an urban society, namely, utilities, housing, roads, schools, and medical and welfare services. Balanced development suggests a more equal distribution of the wealth and therefore an increased purchasing power of the many for the products produced by the economic development.

Again Rhodes states:

> In 1961–1965, Mexico's gross national product increased at about 6 per cent a year. If we exclude 1964, which was an exceptionally good year, we find a rate of 4.9 per cent. Figures for growth in manufacturing are 8.1 per cent for 1961–65 and 6.3 per cent with 1964 excluded. This would be adequate if it were not for Mexico's exploding population. On a per capita basis, production has declined from a yearly average increase of 4.4 per cent in the decade 1940–1950 to an average increase of approximately 2.5 per cent in 1959–1965. The investment rate rose to 14.2 per cent in 1956, but plummetted to 1.6 per cent in 1959, perhaps because markets for consumer goods were not expanding fast enough to attract private capital. The economy appears to have entered a period of relative stagnation. [Rhodes, 1969:27]

Mexico's population is also shifting dramatically. The internal migrations reveal that large percentages of the rural poor are moving into the urban areas. The destination of these migrants appears to be in large proportion the Federal District or Mexico City and the northern border cities adjacent to the United States. To be sure, large centers of population such as Guadalajara and Monterrey are receiving many migrants.

If we look at the population growth of the six Mexican border states we see that they have grown at very substantial rates in the period from 1950 to 1960. If we follow the projections for 1980 based on the 1960 population, the population in the six border states will have grown from 3.7 million in 1950 to 13.8 million in 1980 (see Table 12). A more dramatic increase, however, is that which has occurred in the *municipios* (counties) which are immediately on the border. Table 13 presents the increases of population in four of the large *municipios* between 1940 and 1967, suggesting fantastic increases in some of the *municipios* where a major city is located. In 1940 the population in all the *municipios* next to the U.S. border was .9 million, but by 1967 the population had grown to 2.7 million, most of it concentrated in six or seven Mexican cities along the border. Table 12 shows that the 1960 population of the six border states was 5.4 million. Of these, 2.3 million were located in the *municipios* bordering the United States and by 1967 this figure had risen to 2.7 million (see Table 13). If the projection of 13.8 million for 1980 is any indication of what will happen to the border states, we can expect an even greater percentage of increase in population in the counties along the Mexican border and primarily concentrated in six or seven cities.

TABLE 12

POPULATION CHANGE IN THE MEXICAN BORDER STATES
(1950 TO 1960 AND PROJECTIONS TO 1980)

State	1950	1960	Percentage of Change	Projection 1980
Baja California	226,965	520,165	129.1	2,408,100
Chihuahua	846,414	1,226,793	44.9	1,620,000
Coahuila	720,619	907,734	25.9	2,870,700
Nuevo León	740,191	1,024,182	42.6	2,657,600
Sonora	510,607	783,378	53.4	2,085,400
Tamaulipas	718,167	1,024,182	42.6	2,219,000
Total	3,762,963	5,486,434		13,860,800

SOURCE: Mexican Census 1960 and Benitez and Cabrera, 1966:123–175.

The border, then, has become a great magnet attracting millions of people from the interior of Mexico. Employment opportunities in the United States through such devices as the Bracero Program, the commuter situation, and the wetback traffic have greatly added to the power of the magnet and its

TABLE 13
POPULATION INCREASE OF MEXICAN BORDER MUNICIPIOS

Municipio	1940	Years 1960	1967	Percentage of Change
Tijuana	21,977	165,690	347,501	1,481%
Mexicali	44,399	281,362	540,300	1,117%
Juárez	55,024	276,995	501,416	811%
Nuevo Laredo	31,502	96,043	140,818	347%
Total Mexican Border Municipios	976,693	2,363,728	2,709,136	

SOURCE: Unpublished figures U.S. Department of Labor.

attractiveness to unemployed Mexicans. To the extent that Mexico fails in its economic development, in its population control, and in its control of internal migration, social, economic, and population problems on the Mexican side of the border will become even more serious than they have been in the past.

The Mexican Government

Although the Mexican government, to our knowledge, has not encouraged illegal entry into the United States, it was a party to the Bracero Program between 1942 and 1964. There is no question that the Bracero Program, in spite of the contract violations in the United States and the discriminatory practices, particularly in Texas, was beneficial to Mexico in that it did provide employment for large segments of its population, and the nation profited from the dollar input into the economy. It has been argued that the commuter situation is more beneficial to the economy of the United States because of the low wages paid and because commuters tend to spend the majority of their dollars in the United States. There is no question that the Mexican unemployment situation is somewhat relieved by the employment of Mexican commuters in the United States, but the overall effect is probably not as beneficial to Mexico as the Bracero Program was. We would argue also, as we have in

previous chapters, that the wetback traffic is not only not beneficial to Mexico economically, but it produces untold hardships
for Mexican families and that most individuals are probably
worse off after their experience of becoming wetbacks.

Mexico has concentrated its industrial development in and
around the Federal District, with a few major developments
in places like Monterrey. For any number of reasons the economic development of the border area has long been ignored
by Mexico, two of them being the distance from the capital
and the lack of natural resources in the border area. Only
recently has agricultural development been attempted in the
border region and primarily for exportation to the United
States. The Programa Nacional Fronterizo was established a
few years ago with the primary purpose of developing the arts
and crafts and tourism. It is through this program that Mexico
has launched a campaign to beautify the border, encourage
tourism, and try to persuade the border residents to buy Mexican goods rather than American goods. Since most Mexican
goods are produced in and around the Federal District, subsidies have had to be given for the high cost of transporting
goods from central Mexico to the border. Mexico has not succeeded too well in competing with American goods because it
has been felt that in spite of the subsidy American goods are
cheaper and some would argue that they are of higher quality.
Be that as it may, it would appear to us that unofficially the
Mexican government has in fact encouraged the employment
of its citizens in the United States and has attempted (rather
unsuccessfully) to discourage its citizens from buying United
States goods. It seems, then, that along the border region
Mexico wants American dollars to be spent on Mexican goods.

Mexico also has a federal law regarding the emigration of
its citizens. Leaving the country illegally is a violation of this
law and carries stiff penalties. The law would seem to reflect
Mexico's proper concern for its citizens. However, while U.S.
immigration officials, in recognition of the Mexican law, release
expelled illegal aliens to Mexican officials, the aliens are seldom prosecuted under this law.

With the recent increase in the smuggling of wetbacks into
the United States and since many of the smugglers are Mexican citizens, Mexico has seen fit in recent months to attempt
to interfere in the illegal traffic. The *El Paso Times* (Septem-

ber 14, 1969:1A–8A) reported that Mexican undercover agents, posing as laborers and paying from fifty to a hundred dollars to be smuggled into the U.S. in the trunks of automobiles, had cracked a smuggling ring in the Juárez area. This action was evidently a one-shot affair and to the best of our knowledge has not been repeated.

It is our contention however that since the Mexican border is so far away from the seat of government and relatively isolated from the capital, the government has not shown the same concern for this segment of the population that it has for those close to the capital.

Regarding the future development of Mexico, Rhodes (1969:30–33) argues that the recent high investment in irrigation projects for cash crops in three border states has been done with the North American markets in mind and has benefited primarily the large landowners. This investment has meant less aid for Mexico's subsistence sector and may well result in increasing poverty for a large proportion of Mexico's peasantry. He further argues that industrialization would be helped if minimum wages were raised generally and luxury imports were restricted. Rhodes also suggests a strong progressive income tax which would provide the Mexican government with necessary capital for investment in economic development. We would agree with the above statement and further argue that the border region is desperately in need of sound economic development policies.

In this connection a recent federal labor law was passed which went into effect May 1, 1970. It has been labeled the most advanced labor legislation in Latin America (Christman, 1970:16–19). It calls for increased benefits for labor, which include higher overtime and holiday pay, housing, profit-sharing, the right to strike, seniority benefits, fifteen-day year-end bonus, and many other provisions. The intent of the law is to provide greater protection for labor and obviously a broader market base and therefore an increased demand for industrial products. The private sector claims that the law will mean an immediate increase in labor costs of 25 to 30 percent. Organized labor estimates that the increase will be 5 to 15 percent. Some in the private sector think that labor, with this new law, will price itself out of the market.

Prudencio Lopez, president of the CONCAMIN [Confederación de Cámaras Industriales], maintained that "in reality, the arguments of private enterprise had not been considered" when it came to final passage. He said the Law will hamper harmonic economic and social development in the coming years, and will act as a brake against intensified manufacturing investment. Lopez added that, with the new bill, it is very doubtful that Mexico will be able to meet its stated necessities of creating 720,000 new jobs each year just to keep pace with the nation's growing population. "The Law," he said, "just doesn't correspond to national economic reality." [Christman, 1970:16–17]

There are already indications that the benefits for labor may be short-lived as industry turns toward automation and mechanization to avoid the higher labor costs.

Comercio Exterior de Mexico (February, 1970:2–4), a monthly publication of the Banco Nacional de Comercio Exterior, S.A., in looking at Mexico's ecomonic policy for the seventies, states that a number of problems in the sixties, such as unemployment in the rural areas, inadequate expansion of industrial employment possibilities, and the lack of investment and credit resources, as well as the lack of industrial input (fertilizers, farm machinery) hampered the land-reform program once the distributive stage had been completed. It concludes that for the seventies there is a need for measures to increase employment, wages, and to redistribute income. There is also a need for heavier tax collection to provide resources for greater social and productive investment. Other measures must also be taken to increase export income, augment tourist trade income, curtail imports (in particular, redundant imports), and control, on a short-term basis, border imports and tourist spending abroad. The article concludes:

It is particularly encouraging to note that—particularly in 1969 —economic policy measures have been adopted, or drafted, aimed essentially at resolving the economy's long-range needs. The enactment of the new Federal Labor Law, the value added tax bill to replace the present mercantile income tax, and a federal draft bill to tax luxury spending at home and abroad, are all measures in the right direction. Similarly the extraordinary increase in export income and in that derived from tourist trade along the border and into the country shows the effectiveness of measures adopted to augment this type of foreign exchange inflow.

It follows, in conclusion, that Mexico, through the adoption of adequate policies, will be able to meet the development challenge of the seventies and successfully travel through the decade on the road towards a society built by all for the common good. (Banco National de Comercio Exterior, S.A., 1970)

Toward a National Policy

No one can safely undertake to interpret the Southwest's Mexican-American who does not reckon with the Border in its multiple and seemingly contradicting roles: the gateway and the barrier; the attraction and repulsion of people on a mass scale; the offer and the denial of economic opportunity; the mosaic of small plans and the chaos of large design between two sovereign states; the legal formalities and the illegal realities; the favorite platform of presidents for speeches on Good Neighborliness and a mighty development of military power; a bilingual accommodation of fascinating prospects and a backwash of two cultures; a port of entry and a port of missing men.

Because of its complexity and its durable economic and social effects on people far beyond, south and north, the Border requires a closer look, on both sides. (Galarza, Gallegos, Samora, 1969:11)

As we have shown, a number of factors are related to the increase in illegal immigration from Mexico to the United States. It is not necessary to repeat our position, but it is time to suggest certain areas of concern, which, if properly considered, might provide insights and recommendations leading toward the resolution of some of the major problems presented thus far.

Through custom and tradition the border has always been open and has permitted an enormous interchange between the two countries. Mexican and American crossings number in the millions each year. These legal crossings for purposes of visiting, trade, recreation, and work have resulted in the establishment of strong interdependencies among individuals, organizations and institutions in both countries. Officially, governors, mayors, chamber of commerce, businessmen, public health institutions and many others have formed joint international organizations to pursue common goals. The economy of the border region is considered to be one rather than two distinct ones.

To close the border would be difficult, costly, inconvenient and unfeasible.

To better regulate the border to prevent illegal immigration, and the smuggling of persons is feasible and the following suggestions are made for this purpose.

Penalties for Employers

In the first place there is a law (U.S. Congress, 8 U.S.C. § 1324, 1952) which provides that any person who willfully or knowingly conceals, harbors, or shields from detection, in any place including any building or any means of transportation, or who encourages or induces, or attempts to encourage or induce, either directly or indirectly, the entry into the United States of any alien shall be guilty of a felony. Upon conviction he shall be punished by a fine not exceeding $2,000 or by imprisonment for a term not exceeding five years, or both, for each alien in respect to whom the violation occurs. *Provided, however, that for the purposes of this section, employment, including the usual and normal practices incident to employment, shall not be deemed to constitute harboring.* Thus Public Law 283 made importation or harboring of illegal aliens a felony, but "as a concession to agricultural interests, . . . providing employment and the normal practices incident to employment was excluded from punishment under the act" (Greene, 1969a:479). Therefore an employer, or a farmer, or a labor contractor does not have to take any precautions in the employment of illegal entrants since there is no risk involved.

Ruben Salazar who was recently killed in the Chicano Moratorium in Los Angeles, stated the problem cogently: "There is no law against hiring wetbacks. There is only a law against *being* a wetback" (*Los Angeles Times*, April 27, 1970).

In the editorial page of the same paper for the same date the editor raises this question: "ISSUE: It is illegal for a 'wetback' to work in this country, but it is not illegal to hire one. Shouldn't this be corrected?"

Both the article and the editorial go on to discuss a California bill (Senate Bill 1091) introduced by State Senator Lewis R. Sherman (R., Alameda), that would make it a misdemeanor to knowingly hire wetbacks. The penalty suggested was five dollars for each illegal employee.

We would argue that Public Law 283 should be changed to provide penalties for those who hire illegal entrants. It is the employers rather than the aliens who profit from this traffic, and once they were penalized the demand for cheap labor would certainly diminish.

An employer will argue that he has no right to determine citizenship of those whom he hires, nor is it his duty. Some immigration officials would agree that it is very difficult at times to establish the legal status of an alien, even for them, and therefore it might be very difficult for employers to establish this status. A farmer may also argue that he never sees his employees, because he contracts them through a labor contractor. Therefore who is the real employer in a case like this?

There are a number of indicators which suggest the status of an individual. Besides clothing and language, the lack of documentation might be easily determined. If producing documents were to be a prerequisite for employment, one can readily see that Mexican-Americans, as citizens, might be greatly offended by having to produce documentation when it would not be required of other citizens. Although most Americans carry cards of one sort or another for identification, few carry documentation which establishes their citizenship, such as a birth certificate or a passport. Thus, it would seem to be a simple solution for the government to issue cards to all citizens as documentation of their citizenship.

Restrict Social Security Cards

Almost anyone in this country can get a Social Security card by merely applying for it. Many illegal aliens use this card as identification. Sheldon Greene suggests:

> If the flow of wetback labor is to be controlled, remedial legislation is imperative. The Social Security Act should be amended to provide that if the agency has reasonable cause to believe that a person is not lawfully in the country, the applicant can be required to present indicia of legal residence prior to the issuance of the Social Security card. Such indicia might be a driver's license and/or the Alien Registration card possessed by every

alien entitled to work in the United States under the Immigration and Naturalization laws. [Greene, 1969a:481]

We would agree with Greene that the Social Security Act should be amended. We would disagree that a driver's license is sufficient indicia of legal residence. The citizenship card which we propose would be indicia of both legal residence and citizenship.

Minimum Wages

If effective minimum-wage legislation were enacted in such a way that states would have to comply with it, and particularly in agriculture in such states as Texas, then presumably American citizens could compete effectively with illegal and legal aliens for employment which pays a reasonable wage.

Blanket minimum wage legislation, regardless of types of occupation, products produced, or services rendered and not restricted to interstate commerce would do much to alleviate the unfair competition between citizen and alien. All things being equal, presumably the labor of citizens would be preferred over that of aliens.

Immigration and Naturalization Service

Increased prosecution of aliens who are here illegally could be a deterrent to further entrance. This of course would require an enormous increase in the budget of the Immigration and Naturalization Service, it would require an increase in personnel, and it would require an increase in the detention facilities, including the federal prisons.

Because of the high volume of immigration violations most prosecutions in the Southwest are limited to cases involving deportation violations, smuggling, or falsification of documents. Most of the sentences are light and most are suspended.

If the number of aliens apprehended is related to the size and strength of the Border Patrol, then presumably an increase in the budget and an increase in the authorization of personnel would mean more efficiency in apprehension of illegal aliens. This determination, however, has to be made by Congress.

Restrict Labor Certification

Temporary foreign labor can be imported when the Department of Labor so certifies it. In order to certify such labor an employer must satisfy criteria which indicate that recruitment of domestic workers has been attempted and such workers are not available. The Bureau of Employment Security must conduct an independent investigation for the same determination. It must also determine whether the employer has offered domestic workers housing, workmen's compensation insurance, an established amount of work during the period of the contract, and the particular wages. If the Immigration and Naturalization Service notifies the Labor Department that the employer has hired illegal entrants, this is a ground for refusal to certify the foreign labor. Two recent investigations by the California Rural Legal Assistance suggest that the Department of Labor does not follow its own criteria, to the detriment of the domestic farm worker (Greene, 1969:478).

Prosecution of Aliens

In 1969, 240,958 aliens (I & N Service, 1969, unpublished, Table 24A), the majority of whom were Mexican citizens, were required to depart from the U.S. Of that number 10,505 were deported, 6,845 of whom were Mexicans (I & N Service, 1969, unpublished, Table 24B). The convictions for immigration and nationality violations in 1969 totaled only 4,623. (See Table 14).

The number of aliens apprehended between 1961–1969 totaled 1,263,003, of whom 1,110,661 were expelled (I & N Service, 1969, unpublished, Table 23). This represents aliens from all countries. The convictions for immigration and nationality violations, 1960–1969, totaled 30,460 (also representing aliens from all countries). (See Table 14.) These figures suggest the enormity of the problem and the ease with which aliens can come in and out of the country, presumably without any great danger of penalties.

From their own experience and from the experience of others, most wetbacks who have been apprehended and who have therefore passed through the detention centers appreciate the fact that not many penalties will befall them until

TABLE 14

Convictions for Immigration and Nationality Violations: Years Ended June 30, 1960–1969

Violation	1960–1969	1960	1961	1962	1963	1964	1965	1966	1967	1968	1969
Total	30,460	2,557	2,540	2,530	2,668	2,882	3,442	3,195	3,362	2,661	4,623
Immigration violations	27,707	2,400	2,371	2,357	2,472	2,592	3,037	2,887	3,046	2,420	4,125
Illegal entries	4,068	492	373	256	222	154	190	357	487	440	1,097
Reentries of deported aliens	15,120	1,328	1,375	1,547	1,761	1,820	1,696	1,476	1,619	1,085	1,413
Bringing in or harboring certain aliens	2,654	212	186	133	135	160	177	371	322	395	563
Fraudulent or false documents	512	50	56	76	44	52	28	33	11	48	114
Other fraud or false statements	4,024	144	160	183	167	265	864	509	509	360	863
Alien registration or alien address violations	32	12	6	4	2	2	1	2	3	–	–
Alien crewmen who remained longer	494	68	129	57	49	22	13	83	41	25	7
Stowaways on vessels or aircraft	39	9	14	6	7	2	–	1	–	–	–
Perjury	20	10	6	1	1	1	–	–	–	–	1
Importation of aliens for immoral purposes	6	–	1	2	2	–	1	–	–	–	–
All other violations	738	75	65	92	82	114	67	55	54	67	67
Nationality violations	2,753	157	169	173	196	290	405	308	316	241	498
False representation as citizens of the United States	2,715	150	158	165	195	286	401	307	315	241	497
Other fraud or false statements	38	7	11	8	1	4	4	1	1	–	1

Source: United States Department of Justice, Immigration and Naturalization Service (unpublished, Table 54).

their third apprehension; and even then they will most likely be given a suspended sentence if in fact they go through deportation procedures. The odds for conviction for violating the immigration and nationality laws are not great.

A crackdown on such violations would at first be most expensive because of the need for increased personnel, detention facilities, and court proceedings, but in the long run, in conjunction with the other recommendations suggested, it might prove most effective in reducing the violations.

Prosecution of Smugglers

The prosecution of those persons who make a business of smuggling aliens .has been most lenient and not unlike the prosecution of the alien himself. It is no wonder, then, that since 1965 there has been more than a fourfold increase in the number of smugglers who have been caught. Smugglers have not faired badly before the courts. This has been a lucrative business and the risks have been small. As more and more tragedies occur, we can expect greater penalties from the courts.

We would recommend a crackdown on smugglers who traffic in human lives.

Border-Crossing Card

One of the easiest ways of coming across the Mexican border legally, as we have discussed in a previous chapter, is to enter with a non-resident alien border-crossing card. This card entitles the Mexican citizen to remain in the United States for seventy-two hours and no record is made of the date of entry or the date of departure. Until recently the card was valid for only four years, but now they are considered to be valid indefinitely. Previously the border-crossing card permitted the alien to visit for business or pleasure within 150 miles from the border. A new regulation by the Immigration and Naturalization Service changed this, and now the area is limited to twenty-five miles from the border. In order to travel beyond the twenty-five miles an additional document reflecting the date of entry and the place of admission must be secured. It is estimated that 1,250,000 new cards are outstanding (Greene, 1969a:482). It is also stated that thousands of these cards are issued monthly at all border-crossing points, and hundreds are revoked monthly because of violations. Most people who use these cards legally for entry but who wish to work illegally, thus violating the conditions of the issuance of the card, need but to cross the border and then mail their border-crossing card to their residence or send it by courier. If he is apprehended the alien can claim that he entered without inspection, and when he is expelled from the country he can pick up the card at home and then reenter. Table 15 shows the number of deportable Mexican aliens who were apprehended in 1969. Those who admitted being visitors totaled 28,430. Those without inspection totaled 161,673. It would seem that many thousands of aliens enter with the visitor's permit, but fail to declare it when apprehended.

Greene suggests the following:

> Admittedly, an illegal entrant might be apprehended in a round-up of wetbacks beyond the border area and be returned for having exceeded the geographical limit imposed on his visit; however, to date, no means exists to determine whether he has exceeded the 72-hour period. Curtailment of this abuse could be achieved by limiting visas or other documents of entry to one year and providing that all documents of entry must be stamped with dates of entry and departure for the purpose of ascertaining whether or not the term of stay has been violated. [Greene, 1969a:483]

TABLE 15

Deportable Mexican Aliens, by Status at Entry
Year Ending June 30, 1969

Status	Number
Number located	201,636
Agricultural worker	29
Visitor	28,430
Student	286
Crewman	134
Immigrant	1,662
Stowaway	2
Entry without inspection	161,673
Other	9,420

Source: Table 27B, U.S. Department of Justice, Immigration and Naturalization Service, Unpublished.

Summary and Conclusion

The insatiable demand for cheap labor in the U.S., Mexico's high population growth rate, its insufficient economic development, and its patterns of internal migration are behind the wetback phenomenon.

The U.S. and Mexico created the wetback (and the green-card commuter and the bracero) and both governments must seek a solution to the problem.

Resurrecting the Bracero Program is not a solution, as many think. At the last meeting between Mr. Diaz-Ordaz, outgoing President of Mexico, and Mr. Nixon, it was reported that this possibility was discussed. Our contention is that a Bracero Program is great for U.S. employers and no one else. Such a program certainly does not solve the wetbacks' problem, as was shown earlier.

Only a several-pronged attack to the problem will approach a solution. For the U.S. this means fining employers of illegal aliens, revising regulations concerning social security cards, establishing minimum wages and a citizenship card, expanding the Immigration and Naturalization Service, restricting labor certification, more effective prosecution of aliens and smugglers of aliens, and restricting the issuance of border-crossing permits as well as keeping a record of their use.

For Mexico this means increased efforts in population control and an effective and realistic economic development policy, particularly on its northern border.

Bibliography

BANCO NACIONAL DE COMERCIO EXTERIOR, S. A.
    1970. "Mexico's Economic Policy for the Seventies." *Commercio Exterior de México*, vol. 16, February, pp. 2–4.

BECKER, HOWARD S.
    1958. "Problems of Inference and Proof in Participant Observation." *American Sociological Review* 23: 652–660.

BENÍTEZ, Z. RAÚL, AND CABRERA, A. GUSTAVO.
    1966. *Proyecciones De La Población De México, 1960–1980.* México, D. F.: Banco De México, S. A.

BURMA, JOHN H.
    1954. *Spanish Speaking Groups in the United States.* Durham, N. C.: Duke University Press.

CHRISTMAN, JOHN H.
    1970. "Industry Awaits Impact of New Labor Law." *Mexican-American Review* 38:2.

CHOLDIN, HARVEY M., AND TROUT, GRAFTON D., JR.
    1969. "Mexican-Americans in Transition: Migration and Employment in Michigan Cities," Draft—Final Report, Agricultural Experiment Station, Michigan State University (July).

CLENDENEN, CLARENCE C.
    1969. *Blood on the Border: The United States Army and the Mexican Irregulars.* New York: Macmillan.

DILLINGHAM COMMISSION.
    1911. *Abstracts of Reports of the Immigration Commission*, vol. I, 61st Cong., Senate Document no. 747, Washington, D. C.: Government Printing Office.

147

GALARZA, ERNESTO.
  1964. *Merchants of Labor: The Mexican Bracero History.* Santa
    Barbara: McNally and Loftin.
GALARZA, ERNESTO; GALLEGOS, HERMAN; AND SAMORA, JULIAN.
  1969. *Mexican Americans in the Southwest.* Santa Barbara:
    McNally and Loftin.
GAMIO, MANUEL.
  1930. *Mexican Immigration to the United States.* Chicago: Uni-
    versity of Chicago Press.
GREBLER, LEO.
  1966. *Mexican Immigration to the United States: The Record
    and Its Implications.* Mexican American Study Project;
    Advance Report no. 2, University of California at Los
    Angeles.
GREENE, SHELDON L.
  1969a. "Immigration Law and Rural Poverty—The Problems of
    the Illegal Entrant." *Duke Law Journal,* vol. 1969, no. 3,
    pp. 475–494.
GREENE, SHELDON L.
  1969b. "Wetbacks, Growers and Poverty." *The Nation,* October
    20, pp. 403–406.
HADLEY, ELEANOR M.
  1956. "A Critical Analysis of The Wetback Problem." *Law and
    Contemporary Problems* 21: 334–357.
HANCOCK, RICHARD H.
  1959. *The Role of the Bracero in the Economic and Culture
    Dynamics of Mexico: A Case Study of Chihuahua.* Stan-
    ford: Hispanic American Society.
HELLER, CELIA S.
  1970. "Chicano is Beautiful." *Commonweal* 91: 453–458.
HORGAN, PAUL.
  1954. *Great River: The Rio Grande in North American History.*
    2 vols. New York: Rinehart.
IMMIGRATION AND NATURALIZATION SERVICE.
  1969. Unpublished Tables, p. 15.
KELLY, WILLARD F.
  1954. "The Wetback Issue." *I & N Reporter* 2, no. 3, (January).
LEIBSON, ART.
  1949. "The Wetback Invasion." In "Wetbacks: A Preliminary
    Report to the Advisory Committee; Study of Spanish-

Speaking People," ed. G. I. Sanchez and Lyle Saunders, pp. 10–26. Mimeographed. Austin: University of Texas.

McCarran, Senator Pat.

1953. "Appropriation Hearings Before the Subcommittee of the Senate Committee of the Judiciary of S. 1917." U.S. 83rd Congress, 1st sess.

McLean, Robert N.

1930. "Tighten the Mexican Border." *Survey* 64, no. 1, p. 28.

McWilliams, Carey.

1949. *North From Mexico*. Philadelphia: Lippincott.

Mexican Fact Finding Committee.

1930. *Mexicans in California*. Sacramento, Calif.: State Printing Office.

Montavon, W. G.

1930. "The Economic and Social Background of the Mexican in the United States." In *Sixteenth National Conference of Catholic Charities* (proceedings), p. 272. Washington, D. C.

Morrison, Ethel Mae.

1929. "A History of Recent Legislative Proposals Concerning Mexican Immigration." Master's Thesis, University of Southern California.

North, David S.

1970. *The Border Crossers: People Who Live in Mexico and Work in the United States*. Washington, D. C.: Trans-Century Company.

Panunzio, Constantine.

1933. *How Mexicans Earn and Live*. Berkeley: University of California Press.

Pax, Frank X.

1948. *Mexican-Americans in Chicago*. Chicago: Chicago Council of Social Agencies.

Price, John A.

1969. "The Urbanization of Mexico's Northern Border States." Unpublished paper prepared for the U. S.-Mexico Border Studies Project, University of Notre Dame, Notre Dame, Indiana.

President's Commission on Migratory Labor.

1951. *Migratory Labor in American Agriculture*.

RASMUSSEN, WAYNE D.
   1951. *A History of the Emergency Farm Labor Supply Program 1943–1947*. Agricultural Monograph, no. 13, United States Department of Agriculture, Bureau of Agricultural Economics, Washington, D. C.
RHODES, ROBERT I.
   1969. "The Future of Mexican Development." *Vidya: Journal of the Regional Council for International Education* 3, Spring, pp. 23–33.
RHODES, ROBERT I.
   1970. "Mexico—A Model For Capitalist Development in Latin America?" *Science and Society* 34, no. 1, pp. 61–77.
RUNGELING, BRIAN S.
   1969. "Impact of the Mexican Alien Commuter on the Apparel Industry of El Paso, Texas." Ph.D. Dissertation, University of Kentucky.
SALAZAR, RUBEN.
   1970. *Los Angeles Times*, April 27, p. 12.
SAMORA, JULIAN, ED.
   1966. *La Raza: Forgotten Americans*. Notre Dame, Ind.: University of Notre Dame Press.
SAMORA, JULIAN, AND BUSTAMANTE, JORGE A.
   1970. "Mexican Immigration and American Labor Demands." Manuscript read at The Center for Migration Studies Conference on Labor and Migration, March 13–14, at Brooklyn College, Brooklyn, New York.
SANCHEZ, GEORGE I.
   1949. "The Wetback Problem of the Southwest." In "Wetbacks: A Preliminary Report to the Advisory Committee; Study of Spanish-Speaking People," ed. G. I. Sanchez and Lyle Saunders, pp. 27–30. Mimeographed. Austin: University of Texas.
SANCHEZ, GEORGE I., AND SAUNDERS, LYLE, EDS.
   1949. "Wetbacks: A Preliminary Report to the Advisory Committee; Study of Spanish-Speaking People." Mimeographed. Austin: University of Texas.
SAUNDERS, LYLE.
   1950. "The Social History of Spanish-Speaking People in Southwestern United States Since 1846." Paper delivered at 4th Regional Conference, Southwest Council on Education of Spanish-Speaking People, January 23–25.

SAUNDERS, LYLE.
  1951. "Sociological Study of the Wetbacks in the Lower Rio Grande Valley." Paper read at the 5th Annual Conference Southwest Council on the Education of Spanish-Speaking People, George Pepperdine College, Los Angeles.
SAUNDERS, LYLE, AND LEONARD, OLEN E.
  1951. "The Wetback in the Lower Rio Grande Valley of Texas." Inter-American Education—Occasional Paper VII, University of Texas, Austin.
SCHMIDT, FRED.
  1970. A paper analyzing the economy on the U.S. side of the border, prepared for the U.S.-Mexico Border Studies Project, University of Notre Dame, Notre Dame, Ind.
SCHUTZ, ALFRED.
  1967. *The Phenomenology of the Social World,* trans. by George Walsh and Frederick Lehenert. Evanston, Ill.: Northwestern University Press.
SCRUGGS, OTEY M.
  1961. "The United States, Mexico and the Wetbacks, 1942–1947." *Pacific Historical Review,* May, pp. 149–164.
SCRUGGS, OTEY M.
  1963. "Texas and the Bracero Program, 1942–1947." *Pacific Historical Review,* August, pp. 251–264.
SENATE COMMITTEE ON LABOR AND PUBLIC WELFARE.
  1969–1970. "Migrant and Seasonal Farmwork Powerlessness." Citation from the Hearings of the Senate Subcommittee on Migratory Labor of the Senate Committee on Labor and Public Welfare, 90th Cong., 1st and 2nd sess., Part V, Border Commuter Labor Problems.
SILVERTON, DORIS.
  1970. "The Mexican Maid." *McCall's* 98, no. 1 (October).
SPOTA, LUIS.
  1962. *Murieron a Mitad Del Rio.* Libro-Mex. Editores, Mexico.
SWING, J. M.
  1955. "A Workable Labor Program." *I & N Reporter* 4, no. 2 (November).
TEXAS STATE BUREAU OF LABOR STATISTICS.
  1959. *Laws of Texas Relating to Labor.* Austin, Texas.
THOMPSON, WARREN S.
  1937. *Research Memorandum on Internal Migration in the Depression.* Studies in the Social Aspects of the Depression. New York: Social Science Research Council.

UNITED STATES BUREAU OF IMMIGRATION.

    1903. *Annual Report,* Washington, D. C.

UNITED STATES CONGRESS

    1952. Law 8 U. S. C. § 1324, (p. 11).

UNITED STATES CONGRESS

    1926. *Hearings Before the Committee on Immigration and Naturalization, Seasonal Agricultural Laborers From Mexico,* 69th Cong., 1st sess., Washington, D. C.: Government Printing Office.

UNITED STATES DEPARTMENT OF JUSTICE.

    Annual Report of the Immigration and Naturalization Service. Washington, D. C.

UNITED STATES DEPARTMENT OF JUSTICE.

    1969. Part I. The Judiciary. Departments of State, Justice, and Commerce, The Judiciary, and related agencies, Appropriations for 1970. Hearings before a Subcommittee of the Committee on Appropriations, House of Representatives, 91st Cong., 1st sess.

UNITED STATES DEPARTMENT OF LABOR.

    Annual Report of the Commissioner General of Immigration. Washington, D. C.: Government Printing Office.

UNITED STATES DEPARTMENT OF LABOR.

    Annual Report of the Secretary of Labor. Washington, D. C.: Government Printing Office.

WESTERN HEMISPHERE IMMIGRATION HEARINGS.

    1968. *The Impact of Commuter Aliens Along the Mexican and Canadian Borders,* Hearings of the Select Committee on Western Hemisphere Immigration. Part I, El Paso, Tex.; Part II, San Diego, Calif.; Part III, Brownsville, Tex.; Part IV, Detroit, Mich. Washington, D. C.: Government Printing Office.

WESTERN HEMISPHERE IMMIGRATION HEARINGS.

    1968. *The Report of the Select Commission on Western Hemisphere Immigration.* Washington, D. C.: Government Printing Office.

Appendix I

This material, which is cited throughout the volume, is part of a series of official responses from the Immigration and Naturalization Service to a number of questions put to them by the Senate Committee on Labor and Public Welfare, as part of their hearings on "Migrant and Seasonal Farmwork Powerlessness."

The reference to these questions and answers is as follows: the Senate Committee on Labor and Public Welfare, 1969–1970. "Migrant and Seasonal Farmwork Powerlessness." Citation from the Hearings of The Senate Subcommittee on Migratory Labor of the Senate Committee on Labor and Public Welfare, 90th Congress, 1st and 2nd Sessions, Part V, Border Commuter Labor Problems.

Subcommittee Inquiry

1. Would you please explain all of the different ways by which persons enter the United States from Mexico? What, exactly, is the statutory, historic, or other basis for:

a. U.S. citizens commuting daily from Mexico (using birth or baptismal certificates or other documents)?

b. temporary visitors (3 day passes)?

c. Alien commuters (daily green card commuters)?

d. permanent resident alien commuters (seasonal green card commuters)?

f. foreign contract workers?

g. any other?

RESPONSE

a. Immigration authorities are empowered to exclude aliens only. The exclusion provisions of immigration laws are concerned exclusively with aliens. However, every person seeking to enter the United States is presumptively deemed an alien, until he produces evidence to remove himself from that category. *U.S.* v. *Sing Tuck,* 194 U.S. 161, 169, 24 S.Ct. 621. 48 L. Ed. 917 (1904). A person who satisfactorily establishes that he is a citizen of the United States cannot be barred from entering the United States. *Worthy* v. *U.S.,* 328 F. 2d 386 (C.A.5, 1964). This right of entry may be claimed by any citizen of the United States, including those who do not reside in this country.

The following documents, in possession of the rightful holder, constitute prima facie evidence of United States citizenship:

United States Passport
birth certificate
baptismal certificate
certificate of naturalization
certificate of citizenship
Identification Card (I-179)
Identification Card (I-197)
State Department Report of Birth Abroad (FS-240)
State Department Certificate of Identity (FS-225)
State Department Card of Identity (FS-255-A)
U. S. Coast Guard Merchant Marines Document (CG-2838)
Air Crewman Identification Card

Under 22 CFR 53.2(b), however, a United States citizen who is travelling between Mexico and the United States ordinarily is not required to bear a valid U.S. passport to enter or depart from the United States. Consequently, applicants claiming United States citizenship at the Mexican border can substantiate their claim by presenting one of the foregoing documents or by any other evidence which satisfies the immigration officer.

b. Section 101(a)(15)(B) of the Immigration and Nationality Act (8 USC 1101[a][15][B]) classifies as a nonimmigrant an alien who is visiting the United States temporarily for business or pleasure. Section 212(a)(26) of that Act (8 USC 1182[a][26]) makes a nonimmigrant excludable if he is not in possession of a valid passport and a valid nonimmigrant visa or border crossing identification card. Section 101(a)(6) of the Act (8 USC 1101[a][6]) defines a border crossing identification card as "a document of identity bearing that designation issued to an alien . . . who is a resident in foreign contiguous territory, by a consular officer, or an immigration officer for the purpose of crossing over the border between the United States and foreign contiguous territory in accordance with such conditions for its issuance and use as may be prescribed by regulations."

Section 212(d)(4)(B) of the Act (8 USC 1182[d][4][B]) authorizes the Secretary of State and the Attorney General to waive the passport and visa requirement of section 212(a)(26) with respect to nationals of foreign contiguous territory or adjacent islands, on the basis of reciprocity.

Under section 214 of the Act (8 USC 1184), the admission of a nonimmigrant is for such time and under such conditions as the Attorney General may by regulations prescribe.

Under regulations of the Immigration and Naturalization Service (8 CFR 212.1[c]) and the Department of State (22 CFR 41.6[c]) the visa and passport requirement is waived for a Mexican national applying for admission from contiguous territory as a temporary visitor who is in possession of a Nonresident Mexican Border Crossing Identification Card (Form I-186).

Upon approval of an application for issuance of Form I-186, that card may be issued by a consular officer at a United States consular post in the interior of Mexico or by a United States immigration officer at a port of entry at the Mexican border. Pursuant to 8 CFR 212.6(a), the rightful holder of a Form I-186 applying for admission as a temporary visitor at the Mexican border may be admitted without further documentation if he will remain in the United States no longer than 72 hours and will not proceed beyond 25 miles from the border. If he intends to stay within the 25-mile distance from the border for more than 72 hours but not more than 15 days, or he intends to visit beyond the 25-mile distance but within the State of California, Arizona, New Mexico or Texas for not more than 15 days, he is issued a Form SW-434 upon admission. If he wants to remain more than 15 days or to proceed beyond the four border states he is issued Form I-94 (Arrival-Departure Record) upon admission.

c. The daily commuter is an alien who resides in a contiguous foreign country and who crosses the border daily or several times a week to stable employment in the United States. This is a special status under the immigration laws, with deep historical roots.

Until 1921 there were no numerical limitations on immigration, and aliens were free to come to employment in this country, if they did not infringe the contract labor restrictions or the other exclusions of the immigration laws, Numerical limitations on immigration were introduced in 1921, but those restrictions did not apply to aliens who had been in Canada or Mexico for one year, section 2(a)(7), act of May 19, 1921, 42 Stat. 5, a period raised to five years by section 2 of the act of May 11, 1922, 42 Stat. 540.

The temporary legislation of 1921 was succeeded by the act of May 26, 1924, 43 Stat. 153, which established a permanent system of quota allocation and control. Natives of Western Hemisphere countries were excepted from quota limitations, although immigrants from those countries were required to obtain and present immigration visas or equivalent documents. But the most significant innovation relating to the border-crossing workers was the system of classifying entrant aliens as immigrants and nonimmigrants. Immigrants were defined as all entrants except certain designated nonimmigrant classes coming temporarily. Among the designated nonimmigrant classes were temporary visitors "for business or pleasure." Section 3, act of May 26, 1924, 43 Stat. 153.

In administering the 1924 act, commuters first were considered temporary visitors "for business" and were free to continue to come to their employment in this country. However, on April 1, 1927, the immigration authorities promulgated General Order 86 which reversed their former position and declared that aliens coming to work were not temporary visitors "for business" but were classified as immigrants. This interpretation was upheld by the Supreme Court in *Karnuth* v. *Albro*, 279 U.S. 231, 242–244, 1929, which found that the statutory reference to business was limited to "intercourse of a commercial character."

In studying the problem at that time the immigration authorities concluded that Congress had not intended to interfere with the established pattern of regular border crossings by workers from adjacent countries who commuted to jobs in the United States. Such aliens, almost without exception, could obtain immigrant visas without difficulty. But they would be faced with an impossible task if they were required to obtain a new visa for each daily reentry. Therefore, the immigration authorities devised a border-crossing identification card which could be obtained by aliens who frequently crossed the international boundary. Such cards were issued to immigrants and nonimmigrants. Rule 3, subdivision Q, paragraph 1, Immigration Rules of March 1, 1927 and January 1, 1930. Their issuance and use later received express sanction in section 30 of the Alien Registration Act of 1940, 54 Stat. 673.

Thus, a commuter was able to procure an immigrant visa and lawful admission as an immigrant. Thereafter he would obtain a border-crossing identification card, and with that card was admitted each day as returning to his immigrant status in the United States. This arrangement was in harmony with the good neighbor policy with Canada and Mexico endorsed in the provisions of the 1924 act which conferred nonquota status on persons born in those countries. Moreover, it facilitated travel across the Canadian and Mexican borders and avoided serious dislocations in the border areas.

The commuter program was well known to Congress and was discussed and endorsed, at least implicitly, in the comprehensive study by the Senate Judiciary Committee which preceded the 1952 act. This was in the Senate Report 1515 of the 81st Congress, second session, at page 535.

Nothing in the Immigration and Nationality Act or its legislative antecedents indicated that Congress was dissatisfied with this program or desired to change it in any way. Like the 1924 act, the 1952 legislation did not define "immigrant," except to specify that every alien was an immigrant who was not within the nonimmigrant classes. Section 101(a)(15), Immigration and Nationality Act, 8 USC 1101(a)(15).

In determining those who are at a given time to be deemed immigrants care must be taken to avoid the requirement of "residence," domicile," or place of "abode," since by specific definition an immigrant is any alien not a nonimmigrant, without regard to place of residence, domicile, or abode. The right to reenter the United States to continue a prior status after a temporary absence is accorded to those who have been "lawfully admitted for permanent residence." This is found in section 101(a)(27)(B), Immigration and Nationality Act, 8 USC 1101(a)(27(B), and that term is defined as "the status of having been lawfully accorded the privilege of residing permanently in the United States." Section 101(a)(20), Immigration and Nationality Act, 8 USC 1101(a)(20). It is significant that this statute speaks of one who has been accorded the privilege of residence and does not require that the person having that status must actually reside here.

Thus, the congressional definition has been deemed to coincide with the long established administrative interpretation as reflected in the commuter program.

After enactment of the 1952 Act the Immigration and Naturalization Service concluded that no change in the commuter program was intended and that program continued thereafter without interruption. Its continuing validity was endorsed by the Board of Immigration Appeals in the *Matter of H. O.*, 5 I. & N. Dec. 716 (1954).

Subsequent to the enactment of the Immigration and Nationality Act there was litigation challenging the validity of the alien commuter program. Particularly, it was contended that section 212(a) (14), Immigration and Nationality Act, 8 USC 1182(a)(14), could bar the admission of commuters, notwithstanding that returning lawful resident aliens are unquestionably exempted from the operation of that section. In *Amalgamated Meat Cutters* v. *Rogers*, 186 F. Supp. 114 (D.C., 1960) the court held that commuters were not lawful permanent residents for the purpose of section 212(a)(14) when the Secretary of Labor had issued an adverse certification against the employer under the section as it read (66 Stat. 183) prior to its amendment in 1965. This ruling was not appealed, since it had virtually become moot by the time a final judgment was entered. In a later suit challenging the legality of the alien commuter program, *Texas State AFL-CIO* v. *Kennedy*, 330 F.2d 217 (C.A.D.C. 1964), cert. den. 379 U.S. 826, the court dismissed the suit without reaching the merits, holding that the plaintiffs did not have legal standing to sue.

On October 3, 1965 Congress made several amendments to the Immigration and Nationality Act (P.L. 89-236, 79 Stat. 916). Sections 211(b), 8 USC 1181(b) and 212(a)(14), 8 USC 1182(a) (14), were among the sections amended. Subsequent administrative decisions by the Board of Immigration Appeals have concluded that the commuter system continues, unaffected by the 1965 legislation.

Matter of Burciaga-Salecdo, 11 I. & N. Dec. 665 (1966); *Matter of Bonanni,* 11 I. & N. Dec. 791 (1966); Matter of Gerhard, 12, I. & N. Dec. 556 (1967); *Matter of Weindl,* 12 I. & N. Dec. 621 (1968). Since 1965 there have been new court challenges to the validity of the commuter program. In *Gooch v. Clark,* Civil No. 49,500 N.D. Cal., the court, on June 19, 1969 in an unreported decision held that Congress had not abolished the commuter system in 1965 and rejected a challenge to the legality of the program. An appeal is pending before the United States Court of Appeals, Ninth Circuit. A similar suit challenging the legality of the commuter program is *Bustos v. Mitchell,* Civil No. 3386-69, instituted in December 1969 and pending in the United States District Court, District of Columbia.

d. The seasonal worker or seasonal commuter is a relatively new concept under the immigration laws. It developed after the end of the bracero program in 1964, and the status of such aliens has been analogized to that of the daily commuter, discussed in paragraph c., supra. As used here and throughout the responses to the Subcommittee's questions, a seasonal worker or seasonal commuter is an alien lawfully admitted to the United States for permanent residence, who resides in a contiguous foreign country, who comes to the United States solely to perform seasonal work for extended periods, but whose annual stay in the United States is for less than six months. The seasonal worker's situation should be contrasted with that of the resident alien, who is lawfully admitted to the United States and lives in the United States for the preponderance of each year, even though he may spend substantial time in the contiguous country of his origin.

While there has been much discussion and characterization of green card holders as seasonal commuters, experience has demonstrated that few of such workers can be classified as commuters. The difficulty in attempting to designate such aliens as commuters is that the green card worker who comes for seasonal employment usually is physically present in the United States a preponderance of the year in connection with his employment.

e. In addition to illegal entries through surreptitious entry at other than ports of entry, and concealment in vehicles at ports of entry, other methods to affect illegal entry are attempted.

Many persons are intercepted each year attempting entry with counterfeit or altered Alien Registration Receipt Cards (Form I-151), or Mexican Nonresident Alien Border Crossing Cards (Form I-186), or U.S. Citizen Identification Cards (Form I-179) or fraudulent documentation as evidence of employment with Mexican national, state, or municipal governments. Many alien imposters are also intercepted with unaltered stolen or purchased Forms I-151, I-186 or I-179, posing as the rightful holders of those forms. Others attempt illegal entry by falsely claiming United States citizenship, supporting their allegations with various documentation such as stolen or altered or fraudulently obtained birth or baptismal certificates or other documentation, or with false affidavits or testimony. A large number of I-186 holders succeed in effecting entry as temporary visitors, with preconceived intention of working in the United States.

f. The Contract Labor Act of 1885, 23 Stat. 332, was designed to protect workers in this country from competition of imported foreign laborers. Subsequent legislation prior to 1952 continued the prohibition against bringing contract laborers to the United States. By then the contract labor legislation had become obsolete because workers were protected through the strength of the labor union organizations and the advance of social legislation. The contract labor laws were repealed by the Immigration and Nationality Act of 1952, 66 Stat. 279.

Since December 24, 1952, the effective date of the latter Act, the temporary admission of foreign workers has been governed by Sections 101(a)(15)(H) and 214(c) of the Act, 8 USC 1101(a)(15)(H) and 1184(c). The Immigration and Naturalization Service must approve a visa petition by the prospective employer before the temporary worker may be issued an appropriate visa by the consular officer and be admitted to the United States. Two classes of temporary workers are embraced by this section. The first, known as H-1 relates to aliens of distinguished merit and ability coming here temporarily to perform temporary services of an exceptional nature requiring such merit and ability. The second, known as H-2, relates to aliens coming temporarily to the United States to perform other temporary services or labor, if unemployed persons capable of performing such services or labor cannot be found in this country. Foreign contract workers for agricultural employment are usually brought pursuant to the H-2 category.

Under 8 CFR 214.2(h)(2)(ii) the petitioning employer seeking to import H-2 workers is required to submit, as a supporting document with the petition, either a certification from the Secretary of Labor to the effect that qualified persons are not available in the United States to perform the services in question and that the employment of the H-2 workers would not adversely affect the wages and working conditions of workers in the United States similarly employed, or a notice from the Secretary of Labor to the effect that such a certification cannot be issued.

Between 1949 and 1964 large numbers of contract workers, who were known as braceros, were brought from Mexico under special statutory authorization and pursuant to agreement with Mexico. However, Congress ultimately refused to extend this special program, which expired December 31, 1964.

As noted above, the law still permits the importation of agricultural workers from Mexico as H-2 temporary workers, upon petition of the prospective employer, supported by a labor certification. However, the number of labor certifications issued for Mexican agricultural workers has steadily decreased since 1964. As a result, in Fiscal Year 1969 only 229 Mexican agricultural workers were admitted as H-2 nonimmigrants.

g. Members of the following additional classes of persons enter the United States from Mexico:

(1) U.S. citizens who reside in the United States and are returning from temporary visits to Mexico. The comments made in the response to question 1a are pertinent to persons in this class;

(2) immigrants coming to reside in the United States, entering with visas issued by U.S. consular officers pursuant to section 211 of the Act, 8 USC 1201;

(3) nonimmigrants entering with nonimmigrant visas issued by a U.S. consular officer under the various nonimmigrant classifications defined in section 101(a)(15) of the Act, 8 USC 1101 (a) (15). These may include diplomats, visitors, transits, crewmen, treaty traders, students, representatives to international organizations, temporary workers and trainees, information media representatives and exchange visitors;

(4) Mexican local, state and federal government officials entering under a waiver of nonimmigrant visa and passport requirements, in accordance with the authority contained in section 212(d)(4)(B) of the Act, 8 USC 1182(d)(4)(B), and joint regulations of the Service and the Department of State, 8 CFR 212.1(c) and 22 CFR 41.6(c);

(5) lawful permanent resident aliens whose actual residence is in the United States and are returning from a temporary absence. Most of these individuals present Form I-151, which is accepted as a travel document in lieu of a visa pursuant to 8 CFR 211.1(b) (1) if the rightful bearer has been absent not more than one

year. In some instances, he may be admitted if otherwise admissible, upon presentation of an unexpired permit to reenter the United States issued by the Service pursuant to the authority contained in section 223 of the Act, 8 USC 1203, and implementing regulations in 8 CFR 223. When not in possession of either Form I-151 or a permit to reenter, such alien may present a special immigrant visa issued by a U.S. consular officer, classifying the alien as a returning resident within the contemplation of section 101(a)(27)(B) of the Act, 8 USC 1101(a)(27)(B); alternatively a returning resident alien may, as a matter of discretion, be readmitted pursuant to section 211(b) of the Act, 8 USC 1181(b), and 8 CFR 211.1(b)(3) with a waiver of the documentary requirement specified in section 212(a)(20), 8 USC 1182(a)(20), if the district director of the Service having jurisdiction over the port of entry is satisfied there is good reason for the alien's failure to present the required document.

Subcommittee Inquiry

2. How does a person qualify for each of the permits or papers that may be used to cross the border? How does a person qualify for a green card, and what is required to keep a green card once received; for a temporary visitor's card, etc.?

RESPONSE

An alien qualifies for an immigrant visa required by section 211 of the Immigration and Nationality Act, 8 USC 1181, pursuant to 22 CFR 42, which is administered by the Bureau of Security and Consular Affairs, Department of State, and United States consular officers stationed in foreign countries. An application for such an immigrant visa is made to the appropriate United States Consulate in a foreign country, and, if granted, the immigrant visa is issued by the United States Consul.

The responsibility for adjudication of visa petitions to classify an alien as an "immediate relative of a United States citizen" (spouse or child of a U.S. citizen or parent of an adult U.S. citizen), or as a preference immigrant is vested in the Attorney General pursuant to section 204 of that Act, 8 USC 1154. A consular officer may not issue an "immediate relative" or preference immigrant visa until he has been notified by the Immigration and Naturalization Service of the approval of a petition according the immigrant such classification.

An alien who is admitted as an immigrant or who adjusts his status within the United States to that of a lawful permanent resident, is thereafter furnished a laminated Form I-151, Alien Registration Receipt Card, frequently referred to as a "green card." The green card is issued to every alien who has been granted lawful admission for permanent residence. The rightful holder of Form I-151 is entitled to retain it until he either abandons his immigrant status, or is deported, or is naturalized as a United States citizen.

A citizen of Canada, a British subject residing in Canada, and a citizen of Mexico who is seeking entry as a temporary visitor for business or pleasure and is not inadmissible pursuant to 8 USC 1182 may be issued a border crossing card.

A citizen of Canada and British subject residing in Canada make application for a border crossing identification card to an Immigration and Naturalization Service officer at a port of entry on the Canadian border. A citizen of Mexico makes application either to a U.S. consular office in the interior of Mexico, or to a Service office at a port of entry on the Mexican border. Upon approval of the application, the border crossing identification card is issued. The card facilitates inspection and entry of a bona fide visitor for business or pleasure, and is valid until revoked or voided. It may be declared void without notice for violation of immigration laws or indication of inadmissibility.

An alien seeking admission as a nonimmigrant may apply to a consular officer for a nonimmigrant visa. If the consular officer issues the visa pursuant to section 221(a) of the Act, 8 USC 1201(a), the visa is stamped into the alien's passport. The visa is valid for a specific period and for a specific number of entries. It may be revoked by the consular officer or the Secretary of State, in accordance with 8 USC 1201(i).

An application for a reentry permit is submitted prior to departure to the district director of the Service having jurisdiction over the alien's residence in the United States. Upon a determination that the applicant is in fact a lawful permanent resident of this country, that the application is made in good faith, that the alien intends to preserve his lawful permanent residence status after a temporary absence, and that the proposed departure is not contrary to the interests of the United States, the application is approved and the reentry permit is issued by the Service. The permit may be initially valid for no more than one year, and may be extended for no more than one additional year under the terms of section 223 of the Act, 8 USC 1203.

A returning resident alien arriving at a port of entry without documents may apply for admission under a waiver of the documentary requirement. If the district director determines that the applicant is indeed a returning lawful permanent resident, and that there is good reason for failure to have the required document, the district director may grant the waiver.

Subcommittee Inquiry

6. What are the rights and privileges, and obligations and responsibilities, of all classes of border commuters? Can they *vote*, are they subject to the *draft*, must they pay *taxes*, can they collect *social security*, and for what federal programs, such as commodity food, etc., are they eligible?

RESPONSE

Alien commuters have the same rights and privileges in exclusion or deportation proceedings before a special inquiry officer and the Board of Immigration Appeals and courts as other aliens lawfully admitted for permanent residence. They are entitled to the same benefits and subject to the same penalties administered by the Service under the immigration laws as other aliens lawfully admitted for permanent residence.

They are required, as are other aliens lawfully admitted for permanent residence, to notify the Attorney General each January of their current address and of each change of and new address within ten (10) days of such change pursuant to section 265 of the Act, 8 USC 1305.

Whether alien or citizen commuters may vote is a matter for the determination of the political jurisdiction in which they live and work. The applicability of the draft laws and regulations to commuters is a matter within the jurisdiction of the Director, Selective Service System. While at one time that agency considered commuters to be exempt from the draft laws, more recently that agency has reversed that position and now deems them subject to Selective Service requirements.

The applicability of local, state and federal taxes to commuters is a matter within the jurisdiction of those political entities. The Internal Revenue Service has indicated that commuters are subject to federal income tax on income earned in the United States.

Eligibility of commuters for social security benefits or for benefits under other federal programs are matters within the competence of the agencies administering such programs. We are unable to express any view regarding their eligibility for such benefits.

Subcommittee Inquiry

7. It has been established that the daily commuter alien has a different status by administrative regulations than a permanent resident alien because: (1) the commuter alien with a green card (as a visa) may not reenter if he is unemployed in the United States for six months; and (2) he may not enter with the purpose of working at the sight (*sic*) of a work dispute. If this distinction is perpetuated by administrative regulation, *why then* can not an administrative regulation be promulgated which would prevent the commuter alien from coming to this country to work in an area where it would adversely affect the wages and working conditions of United States workers?

RESPONSE

In section 212(a)(14) of the Immigration and Nationality Act, as amended, 8 USC 1182(a)(14) Congress provided specific controls for the protection of American workers. Section 212(a)(14) applies to specified classes of immigrants. This statute is explicitly inapplicable to the alien lawfully admitted for permanent residence who is returning from a temporary absence, as described in section 101(a)-(27)(B). It has been and continues to be the position of the Immigration and Naturalization Service that a commuter is classifiable under the latter section when he is applying for readmission to this country. It is our view that the adoption of a regulation in the manner proposed would be tantamount to extending the provisions of section 212(a)(14) to a class of immigrants whom Congress has excluded from its terms and would be contrary to the law.

On the other hand, it is our view that the so-called strikebreaker regulation (8 CFR 211.1[b] [1]) is within the ambit of authority specifically granted by Congress, in section 211(b) of the Immigration and Nationality Act, 8 USC 1181(b), to define the documents which may be presented by returning resident immigrants, including commuters. We can find no basis for expanding this statutory authority to support the imposition of a positive entry requirement which the statute precludes.

Subcommittee Inquiry

21. It is well known throughout the border area that so-called "wet maids" are numerous and badly underpaid, sometimes getting as little as $8 to $10 a week plus room and board for long, long hours of work. What is the Service doing to change this situation?

RESPONSE

The Service is continuously attempting to identify and expel any alien who is in the United States illegally, including "wet maids." Since the controlling consideration in such cases is the alien's illegal presence in the United States, the Service is discharging its responsibilities by seeking to locate and remove such illegal aliens.

Subcommittee Inquiry

25. Please submit the following information, for each of the past five years, by geographical area:

    a. the number of smugglers of illegal entrants apprehended?
    b. the number of convictions secured?
    c. the kinds of sentences handed out?
    d. what additional legislation or enforcement resources are needed to further control these practices?

RESPONSE

a. (apprehensions)

	1969	1968	1967	1966	1965
	2,048	1,210	1,219	959	525
Northeast Region	119	72	46	41	54
Southeast Region	20	4	8	28	3
Northwest Region	10	6	10	13	8
Southwest Region	1,899	1,128	1,155	877	488

b. (convictions)

	563	395	322	371	177
Northeast Region	3	3	2	5	4
Southeast Region	3	–	6	4	4
Northwest Region	41	41	9	5	8
Southwest Region	516	351	305	357	161

c. (sentences) *

Months	7,447	3,357	2,395	3,286	1,738
Fines	$43,000	$31,500	$13,150	$18,850	$10,550
Northeast Region					
Months	9	30	24	54	87
Fines	—	—	—	$3,000	$750
Southeast Region					
Months	8	—	96	30	66
Fines	$500	—	—	$2,500	$500
Northwest Region					
Months	580	246	84	12	22
Fines	—	$100	$250	$1,000	$100
Southwest Region					
Months	6,850	3,081	2,191	3,190	1,563
Fines	$42,500	$31,400	$12,900	$12,350	$9,200

* Prior to January, 1969, the Service did not collect statistics as to the portion of sentences which were suspended. A review of the sentences imposed in the Southwest Region during the first six months of fiscal year 1969 (July 1968 to Jan. 1, 1969) shows that of the 2,220 months sentences given in 244 cases, 1,806 months were suspended. The average sentences actually imposed was 1.7 months. During the period Jan. 1, 1969 through Mar. 31, 1969, an aggregate of 2,524 months was imposed in 117 such cases, with 937 months suspended. The average sentence actually imposed was 13.6 months. The increased average during the latter period was attributable to the sentences in two aggravated cases: one in San Antonio, Texas involving a smuggling operation in which three aliens died of suffocation in a closed van and the three defendants received a total of 43 years actual sentence; and the other in southern California, where the defendant received a total of 45 years actual sentence.

During the period April, 1969 through June 30, 1969, the aggregate sentences totaled 2,106 months, and were imposed in 155 cases, with 1,812 months suspended. The average sentence actually imposed again dropped to 1.9 months.

d. The present statute directed against aliens smugglers is section 274 of the Immigration and Nationality Act, 8 USC 1324, which prescribes criminal penalties for smuggling, harboring, transporting or inducing illegal entrants. This is a comprehensive statute, which is utilized to attack those engaged in smuggling aliens into the United States. It is an effective tool to accomplish this purpose, and in our view no additional legislation to penalize such smuggling is needed.

Subcommittee Inquiry

27. What is the Service's policy on the acceptance of baptismal certificates as proof of citizenship of commuting citizens?

    a. Are such certificates still acceptable at the Hidalgo bridge?

    b. Is it true that over the past five years, the certificates were accepted at some parts *(sic)*, but not others?

RESPONSE

a. Yes. As indicated in the response to question 1.a., a baptismal record, in possession of the rightful holder, is deemed prima facie evidence of United States citizenship.

b. There is no basis for refusing to consider valid baptismal certificates, showing birth in the United States, if presented by the rightful holder in support of claimed United States citizenship. Any variation from this procedure would have been contrary to Service policy. Where fraud is suspected, the certificates are lifted by the Service to facilitate necessary interrogation, investigation, and indicated action.

Subcommittee Inquiry

28. What is the process by which illegals apprehended by the Service are escorted back to Mexico?

    a. How many are simply transported across the border?

    b. How many are taken into the interior of Mexico?

    c. Were the charter flights from Port Isabel to Central Mexico abandoned at any time in recent years? If so, please explain.

RESPONSE

Following apprehension in the interior of the United States, illegal aliens are transported by Service transport aircraft, Service bus, and chartered bus to Service-operated staging areas—El Centro, California; El Paso, Texas; Port Isabel, Texas—for onward movement to Mexico. Women and children illegally in the United States usually are found near the border and are permitted to return to Mexico voluntarily.

a. During calendar year 1969, about 55,250 Mexican residents were granted voluntary departure to adjacent Mexican ports of entry. These were aliens who have their residence on or in close proximity to the border. Included in this group were 23,000 women and children and a substantial number who were aged and infirm.

b. 129,257 illegal aliens were removed to the interior of Mexico during calendar year 1969.

c. The charter flights from Port Isabel to Central Mexico were discontinued in February 1969. The flights were replaced by a buslift. The buslift permits the Service to move the aliens to the same general area in Mexico at lower cost.

Subcommittee Inquiry

29. With regard to section 212(a)(14) labor certification provisions of the Immigration and Nationality Act:

a. Do the provisions requiring certification of employment apply to all aliens who seek legal entry as permanent residents and whose entry is based on employment providing their financial responsibility? Please explain.

b. Under what circumstances must a commuter show that he has permanent employment? What definition does the Service use for permanent employment?

c. Which aliens are exempt from the provision of section 212(a)(14)?

d. Has the State Department, or the Service, compiled statistics on the number of aliens admitted for permanent residence during each of the last three years who were exempt from the provisions of 212(a)(14)? If so, please provide.

e. How is the exemption established? Please outline the procedure.

f. What instructions have been issued to those officers granting the exemption, particularly as to sufficiency of proof in establishing preference by citizenship of a relative who claims birth in the United States?

RESPONSE

a. No. By its specific terms, section 212(a)(14) is made applicable only to those immigrants who are (a) nonpreference immigrants as described in section 203(a)(8) of the Act; (b) immigrants who have been granted an occupational preference under section 203(a)(3) or (6); and (c) aliens classified as special immigrants under section 101(a)(27)(A) by reason of birth in an independent Western Hemisphere country or the Canal Zone, and their accompanying or following to join spouses and children. An exemption from the certification requirement is prescribed for any Western Hemisphere special immigrant who is the parent, spouse or child of a citizen or lawful permanent resident of the United States. Under the explicit language of the statute, returning lawful residents, designated as special immigrants under section 101(a)(27)(B), are not subject to the labor certification provisions of section 212(a)(14).

b. There is no requirement that a commuter's employment be permanent. However, he must have reasonably regular and stable employment in the United States. In *Matter of Bailey*, 11 I. & N. Dec. 466, the Board of Immigration Appeals, whose decisions are binding on the Service, held that the regularity and frequency of a commuter's temporary employment in the United States could be taken into account in determining whether his employment was stable. The Board found that an alien could be admissible as a returning resident commuter if his employment in this country was reasonably regular and stable, even though such employment is only part-time, is self-employment, is intermittent, or does not require daily entries.

c. Since section 212(a)(14) by its own terms is made applicable only to certain classes of immigrants, it is not applicable to the following classes of aliens:

(1) Nonimmigrants

(2) Western Hemisphere special immigrants who are the parents, spouses or children of citizens or of lawful permanent residents of the United States

(3) special immigrants described in section 101 (a)(27) (B), (C), (D) and (E) (returning lawful residents, former citizens, ministers, employees and former employees of U.S.)

(4) preference immigrants (on basis of relationship to citizens or residents) under section 203(a)(1), (2), (4), (5)

(5) conditional entrants under section 203(a)(7) (refugees)

(6) immediate relatives of United States citizens under section 201(b)

In addition, by regulation (8 CFR 212.8[b] and 22 CFR 42.91[a][14][ii]), the following classes of persons are declared to be exempt from the labor certification requirement:

(1) An alien who establishes he does not intend to seek employment in the United States,

(2) A member of the Armed Forces of the United States,

(3) A spouse or child accompanying or following to join his spouse or parent who either has a labor certification or does not require such certification,

(4) A female alien who intends to marry a citizen or alien lawful permanent resident of the United States, who establishes that she

does not intend to seek employment in the United States and whose fiancé has guaranteed her support,

(5) An alien who will engage in a commercial or agricultural enterprise in which he had invested or is actively in the process of investing a substantial amount of capital,

(6) An alien who establishes satisfactorily that he has been accepted by an institution of learning in the United States, that he will be pursuing a full course of study for at least two full consecutive years, and that he has sufficient financial resources to support himself and will not seek employment during that period.

d.

Year ended June 30:	1967	1968	1969
Immigrants admitted:	361,972	454,448	358,579
Labor certificates issued:	93,324[1]	141,827[1]	102,913[1]
Immigrants exempt from labor certification requirement:	268,648	312,621	255,666

[1] SOURCE: Table A-1; *Immigrant Worker Certification Program,* prepared by the Manpower Administration, U.S. Department of Labor, Fiscal Years 1967, 1968, and 1969.

Data in Table A-1 includes alien workers precertified for permanent employment by the Department of Labor and processed by the Immigration and Naturalization Service and the U.S. Consular Office on the basis of schedules promulgated by the Department of Labor.

NOTE: Usage of the labor certification document will not necessarily fall in the same year as that of immigrant admission because visa numbers may not be immediately available to visa applicants.

e. An immigrant visa is not issued before the applicant has been issued a labor certification or establishes to the satisfaction of the issuing consular officer that he is exempt from the labor certification requirement. Visa issuance is a function of consular officers of the Department of State, and the Immigration and Naturalization Service is not involved in the case of a Mexican native claiming exemption from the labor certification requirement in connection with an application for an immigrant visa, with one exception. That exception is when the alien claims to be an "immediate relative" of a United States citizen (spouse or child of a United States citizen, or parent of an adult United States citizen). In that case, the citizen is required to file a visa petition with the Service to classify the alien as an "immediate relative" and thereby exempt the alien from the numerical limitation of 120,000 per annum applicable to Western Hemisphere immigrants. Documentary evidence of the claimed relationship must be submitted in support of such a petition. The approval of the petition merely serves to classify the alien beneficiary as an "immediate relative." However, since parents, spouses and children of United States citizens are also exempt from the labor certification requirement applicable to Western Hemisphere natives, consular officers may accept the approval of the petition as evidence of the alien beneficiary's exemption from the certification requirement on the basis of his relationship. In other cases the consular officer presumably requires suitable evidence of a claimed exemption from that requirement.

With respect to Eastern Hemisphere natives, Service approval of a visa petition to classify such an alien under the first, second, fourth or fifth preference, or as "an immediate relative," based upon specified relationships to citizens or lawful permanent residents of the United States, is accepted by the consul as evidence that section 212(a)(14) is not applicable. Before approving a visa petition for third or sixth preference (occupational preference), the Service ascertains that the labor certification requirement has been met. The approved petition is forwarded to the consular officer where the beneficiary will apply for his visa.

f. Every immigration officer engaged in examining and adjudicating petitions or applications has received training and instruction in the immigration laws, and in applicable regulations and inspection techniques. These techniques include interrogation of the applicant for admission, and examination of the documents he presents, including the labor certification or evidence of exemption from the certification requirement.

Every alien who seeks to establish immediate relative classification or preference as a relative of a United States citizen or alien lawful permanent resident of the United States, which classification would provide exemption from the labor certification, must have a visa petition filed on his behalf by the citizen or resident alien on Form I-130 (Petition to Classify Status of Alien Relative for Issuance of Immigrant Visa). The instruction on that form must be carried out and the required documentation must be furnished with the petition. No petition may be approved until the examining officer is satisfied that the relationship exists. . . .

Subcommittee Inquiry

31. With regard to the investigation of fraud:

    a. Who is in charge of investigation?

b. How are the offices responsible for the investigations staffed?

c. How many cases of fraud have been uncovered before a visa is issued during the past five years, and in 1960 and 1955?

d. How many cases of fraud have been uncovered after a visa has been issued during the past five years, and in 1960 and 1955?

e. What efforts are made to deter the continuation of the frauds?

RESPONSE

a. Under the executive direction of a regional commissioner, the 37 District Directors of this Service are in charge of investigations within their jurisdiction. In the 18 larger districts they are aided in the discharge of their responsibilities by Assistant District Directors for Investigations.

b. The attached list shows investigators on duty as of December 31, 1969, which shows how our various offices are staffed. Adjustments are made periodically to meet varying workloads. [See page 174.]

c. & d. Service records are not maintained with separate categories for frauds uncovered before and after a visa is issued. The following figures show the number of fraud investigations conducted in the United States during the fiscal years indicated. Fraud investigations were not recorded separately prior to fiscal year 1956:

Fiscal Years	Fraud Investigations Completed
1969	10,231
1968	6,641
1967	5,337
1966	4,967
1965	5,233
1960	3,234
1956	3,182

e. The Service is constantly concerned with combatting frauds. Various programs have been initiated. Operating procedures, which include a vigorous criminal prosecution policy, were established and field offices have been directed to follow them closely. Close liaison is maintained with the Departments of State and Labor, locally and in Washington. Liaison is also maintained with state and local authorities at all levels.

UNITED STATES DEPARTMENT OF JUSTICE
IMMIGRATION AND NATURALIZATION SERVICE
On Duty Force of Investigators—December 31, 1969

Northeast Region

°Burlington	5
°°Boston	16
Providence	1
Springfield	1
°°Buffalo	12
Albany	3
Ogdensburg	1
°°Hartford	8
°°Newark	29
°°New York	136
°Portland, Me.	2
°St. Albans	4

Southeast Region

°Richmond	4
°°Atlanta	4
Memphis	2
°°Baltimore	9
°°Cleveland	11
Cincinnati	3
°Miami	1
Jacksonville	8
Tampa	29
°°New Orleans	136
°°Philadelphia	2
Pittsburgh	4
°San Juan	10
Christiansted	2
St. Thomas	2
°°Washington	13
Norfolk	7
Wilmington	1

Northwest Region

°St. Paul	3
°°Chicago	54
Hammond	6
Milwaukee	5
°°Detroit	18
°°Helena	2
Boise	1
°°Kansas City	4
St. Louis	3
°°Omaha	5
°°Portland, Ore.	14
°°St. Paul	4
°°Seattle	10
Spokane	2

Southwest Region

°San Pedro	4
°°Denver	4
Salt Lake City	3
°°El Paso	11
Albuquerque	1
Marfa	1
°°Honolulu	4
°°Los Angeles	83
Calexico	2
San Diego	7
San Luis Obispo	1
San Ysidro	2
°°Phoenix	4
Nogales	1
San Luis	2
Tucson	2
°°Port Isabel	3
Brownsville	1
Houston	5
°°San Antonio	16
Dallas	6
Del Rio	1
Hidalgo	2
Laredo	2
°°San Francisco	42
Fresno	2
Las Vegas	2
Reno	1
Sacramento	2

°Regional Office
°°District Office

Subcommittee Inquiry

33. With regard to offers of employment:

a. What evidence, conditions, or requirements are required to establish the sufficiency of an offer of employment?

b. Who makes the final determination on sufficiency requirements?

c. What is considered the minimum offer, in order to qualify, for example, for a family of two, three, four, etc., up to ten? Are instructions as to sufficiency different for each immigration district, or each consular area? If so, why, and how are they different?

d. If an offer of employment is suspected of being false, what action is taken? Is any information of this nature ever publicized, and if so, when was the last time? What were the circumstances?

e. Have extensive frauds been uncovered in offers of employment? Who generally engages in such frauds? Give examples.

f. If the fraud is uncovered after the visa is issued, what action is taken? What procedures apply? How many such frauds were uncovered during the past five years?

g. How does a consular office go about trying to prove that a work offer is fraudulent? What procedures are established to cope with this problem?

h. Once a visa has been granted, does either the State Department or the Service conduct any investigations as a matter of course to determine how many offers of employment, both under certification, or under preference, are actually bona fide? Who is responsible for insuring compliance?

i. If so, who conducts such investigations? How many Service personnel are used, for example, in the Los Angeles Immigration district, and how many in the San Antonio district? What instructions do they operate under?

RESPONSE

a. Offers of employment made in connection with visa issuance are considered under two sections of the law. The first, under section 212(a)(14) of the Act, 8 USC 1182(a)(14), is primarily determined by the Labor Department. The second, relating to the "public charge" ground of inadmissibility under 212(a)(15), 8 USC 1182-(a)(15), is primarily determined by the U.S. Consul. Consequently the Service defers to the Labor and State Departments with respect to parts a, b, c and g of this question.

d. The Labor Department has promulgated the following regulation in 29 CFR 60.5: "*Validity*. Certifications issued pursuant to this part are invalid if the representations upon which they are based are incorrect. They are applicable only to the positions as described on Form ES-575B or as defined in the applicable schedule."

Labor certifications presented to the Service with petitions or applications are carefully scrutinized. If found to have been issued on false claims with respect to the conditions of the job offer or the qualifications of the beneficiary, the certification may be declared invalid and the petition or application is denied on the basis that the required certification is lacking. Since July 4, 1967, in accordance with the Freedom of Information Act, the Service has made available in public reading rooms copies of unpublished decisions on various types of petitions and applications. Published decisions may be purchased from the Superintendent of Documents, United States Government Printing Office. Decisions are published when it appears they may be of precedent value and serve as guidance to Service officers, aliens, attorneys and other interested persons.

Examples of decisions where the Service concluded that the petitioner would not employ the beneficiary in the manner set forth in the offer of employment on which the labor certification was based are *Matter of Izdebska*, 12 I. & N. Dec. 54 (1966), and *Matter of Desi*, 11 I. & N. Dec. 817 (1966). Petitions for sixth preference classification were denied in those cases.

Where it comes to Service attention that an alien entered the United States with the preconceived idea of not proceeding to the employment specified in the labor certification presented in support of the immigrant visa, the Service institutes expulsion proceedings on the charge that the alien was inadmissible at the time of entry. See *Matter of Hernandez-Uriarte*, 13 I. & N. Dec. __ (I.D. 1956, 1969); *Matter of Poulin*, 13 I. & N. Dec. __ (I.D. 1973, 1969).

e. Early in calendar year 1966, an increase was noted in the number of complaints from employers who had secured labor certifications for alien employees, particularly live-in domestics, that such employees either failed to appear for the certified positions or shortly after taking the positions departed therefrom and took more lucrative jobs. Investigation disclosed that many of the aliens entered the United States as temporary visitors and then engaged in employment as domestics, in violation of their status, while awaiting processing of applications for labor certifications and immigrant visas. Every effort is made to locate and remove such aliens from the United States as quickly as possible.

Investigation further disclosed widespread abuses in the obtaining of labor certifications. Many aliens, either alone or with assistance of a third party, obtained labor certifications and admission to the United States as immigrants ostensibly to take employment as live-in domestics when, in fact, they were entering to seek employment as sewing machine operators or unskilled factory workers. Some of the live-in domestic labor certifications (which contained numerous mis-representations) were filed as a convenience to the aliens by relatives or friends who were financially unable to pay the required salaries and/or had no actual need for domestics.

f. If any fraud is uncovered, including a fraudulent offer of employment, after the visa is issued but prior to the time the applicant applies for admission as an immigrant at a United States port of entry, the consular officer or the Secretary of State is authorized to revoke the visa pursuant to section 221(i) of the Immigration and Nationality Act, 8 USC 1201(i).

If the alien applies for admission at a United States port of entry in possession of an immigrant visa, and it appears the visa was fraudulently obtained, he would be referred to a Special Inquiry Officer pursuant to sections 235 and 236 of the Act, 8 USC 1225 and 1226, for a hearing on his admissibility, on the ground that the alien appeared to be inadmissible under sections 212(a)(14) and (19) of the Act, 8 USC 1182(a)(14) and (19). The latter sections deal with inadmissibility for lack of a required labor certification and for obtaining a visa by fraud or misrepresentation.

If an alien is admitted to the United States as an immigrant in possession of an immigrant visa, and it is later discovered that he was not eligible for admission at the time of entry because of inadmissibility on the aforementioned grounds, or any other grounds of inadmissibility, the Service may institute deportation proceedings on the charge that the alien is a member of the deportable class specified in section 241(a)(1) of the Act, 8 USC 1251(a)(1). The expulsion hearing is held before a Special Inquiry Officer in accordance with section 242 of the Act, 8 USC 1252.

The Service is unable to furnish statistics on the number of fraudulent offers of employment uncovered during the past five years.

h. On June 2, 1967 an active program against violators was initiated. Provision was made for the publication of precedent decisions involving labor certifications where an alien fails to engage, or only works briefly, in the labor field for which certified, and then moves on to a non-certified position. Field offices were directed to screen recently arrived or currently arriving sixth preference and other immigrant cases, particularly where the record indicates that an immigrant visa was issued on the basis of a live-in domestic labor certification, and to expedite the investigation of selected cases. Deportation proceedings against violators have been brought under section 241(a)(1) of the Immigration and Nationality Act, 8 USC 1251(a)(1).

As a result of this program, precedent decisions have been obtained from the Board of Immigration Appeals which have established clear-cut guidelines for all field offices to follow, thus insuring uniformity in Service efforts to combat violations of the labor certification requirement of section 212(a)(14) of the Act, as amended.

This screening process is continuing. Some offices detected a high incidence of fraud in cases of aliens from certain Central and South American countries who obtained immigrant visas on representations that they were qualified dressmakers, one of the occupations included in the Schedule C—Precertification List, and therefore not required to obtain individual labor certifications under section 212 (a)(14). In order to determine the extent of the fraudulent activity in this area, separate lists were compiled of all alien dressmakers coming from Ecuador, El Salvador and Costa Rica who were admitted as immigrants during the period January through June 1968. The lists were forwarded to the district offices for investigation. Due to the successful results reported, plans were formulated to furnish the Service field offices with similar lists involving other occupations. Lists of tailors and bakers who were admitted as immigrants during specified periods were also forwarded to the district offices of the Service for investigation on November 25, 1969.

The Department of Labor has primary responsibility for the investigation of frauds practiced in the obtaining of labor certifications. This Service has the responsibility to determine if aliens involved in such activities are amenable to exclusion or deportation. After conferences with the Department of Labor, this Service agreed to conduct investigations for the purpose of determining if fraud was involved in the procurement of the labor certification. After investigation, if warranted, the facts are presented to the appropriate United States Attorney for consideration of prosecution of the parties involved for violations under 18 USC 1001. If fraud in obtaining the labor certification is not involved, cases involving possible failure of employers to comply with the terms of their contracts with the aliens are referred to the Department of Labor for such action as is deemed to be appropriate.

i. During fiscal year 1969, 14 investigators completed a total of 2,065 fraud investigations in the Los Angeles district, and 4 investigators completed a total of 284 fraud investigations in the San Antonio district. No separate statistical breakdown is maintained for the various types of investigations mentioned in the Subcommittee's inquiry; they are included in the total of 2,065 and 284 fraud investigations completed in the Los Angeles and San Antonio districts, respectively.

Fraud investigations and other investigations initiated by this Service are conducted for the purpose of establishing whether the alien involved is in the United States in violation of any provisions of the Immigration and Nationality Act and, where appropriate, to establish whether there has been a violation of the criminal statutes under the jurisdiction of this Service.

Subcommittee Inquiry

35. Have many frauds been uncovered in regard to establishing preference by marriage to a citizen, or legal resident spouse? By the birth of a United States citizen child? If so, how many?

    a. How are those cases handled? How many personnel are engaged in investigating this type of case?

    b. How extensive (*sic*) are these cases publicized? Is it fair to conclude that some problems along the border are traceable to permissive policy with regard to enforcement of regulations?

RESPONSE

Service records concerning fraud investigations do not particularize the information requested. See answer to questions 31c and d for total fraud investigations completed during the last five fiscal years.

    a. See answers to questions 31b and 31c and d. Currently there are approximately 73 investigators assigned to all types of fraud investigations. The Service makes every effort to expeditiously conduct all fraud investigations. Particular emphasis is given to the identification and prosecution of third parties who aid the aliens in such activities. Many of the investigations disclosed criminal violations, including conspiracies, involving the aliens and other persons who for substantial fees assisted them in their efforts to circumvent the immigration laws. The principal criminal statutes violated are 18 USC 371 (conspiracy), 18 USC 911 (false claims to United States citizenship), 18 USC 1001 (false statements), and 18 USC 1546 (fraud).

b. The results of this prosecution policy are publicized in American newspapers and in the foreign language news media. We believe this publicity materially assists in the curtailment of these frauds. We are not aware of permissive policy in the enforcement of the regulation, and our answer to the second portion of this question is negative.

Subcommittee Inquiry

39. If his offer is not considered sufficient, and the applicant obtains an offer from someone not certified on strike, can such an applicant after admission, then go to the struck farm and work, alleging that he was not a commuter but a bona fide legal resident when he applied for and obtained work on the struck farm?

a. If such employment is not permissible, what has been done by the Service to insure that no violations have occurred?

b. What instructions have been given to insure that such cases do not occur? Has any publicity been given to this kind of situation? If so, where?

c. How many personnel in the Starr County, Texas, area were assigned to such investigations, if any?

d. In other words, what has the Immigration Service done, as positive action to (1) prevent violations in this respect; (2) implement actual enforcement?

e. At a district level, who has been given the responsibility to take positive enforcement action? What specific action has been taken? How many persons are actually engaged in such action?

f. If checks were made at struck farms, who made the checks for violations? How many checks were made in Starr County during 1968? How many checks were made in the Coachella Valley of California in 1968 and 1969?

g. When the checks were made, what was the procedure used? Was each worker checked individually and were employment records checked? Were the records of truckers under contract or paying piece rates also checked?

RESPONSE

As previously stated, the labor certification applies to the initial entry only. If such an entrant is admitted and then proceeds to a place of employment other than that specified in his labor certification, an investigation is made in order to determine his intent at time of entry. If it is determined that such alien's intent at the time of his admission was to obtain work at a place of employment, whether struck or nonstruck, other than that specified in his labor certification, then deportation proceedings are instituted against him. If the question of intent at the time of entry is resolved in his favor, a lawful permanent resident is not restricted by law or regulation from accepting any employment of his choice. However, if such person acquires commuter status after his admission he becomes subject to 8 CFR 211.1(b)(1).

a. Immediately upon receipt of an announcement by the Secretary of Labor that a labor dispute exists, the ports of entry on the Mexican border are notified and directed to take the necessary steps to implement the regulation. Aliens applying for admission as resident aliens in possession of Forms I-151 entering to work are screened to determine whether they are entering in violation of the regulation. Holders of Form I-151 and residents of Mexico entering the United States to work are furnished lists of locations where it has been certified that labor disputes exist. Announcements are posted at ports of entry advising of restrictions to accepting employment on farms where labor disputes exist. Border Patrol traffic checks and backup stations are also alerted to the labor dispute and begin checking holders of Form I-151 to determine if they are proceeding to employment in areas involved in the labor dispute.

b. Internal instructions have been issued to operating divisions within the Service. As stated above, aliens entering from Mexico to work are advised individually as to restrictions on accepting employment at struck farms, announcements are posted at ports of entry, holders of I-151 encountered in field and traffic checks are furnished lists of farms where labor disputes exist, and Service representatives have met with growers associations and representatives of labor unions and explained the regulations and procedures in detail.

c. Following the announcement by the Secretary of Labor on July 10, 1967, that a labor dispute was in progress on six farms in Starr Country, Texas, Service officers at the ports of entry in the Lower Rio Grande Valley area carefully screened all aliens seeking admission as returning residents with Forms I-151 to insure that none were entering for the purpose of accepting employment at the places where labor disputes existed or of continuing employment at such places which began after July 10. Any alien intercepted at the port who came within the purview of the regulation was refused admission; however, in all known instances such aliens arranged for employment at nonstruck farms and were thus admissible under the regulation. The struck farms have been checked periodically by the Border Patrol. The place of residence of each holder of a Form I-151 was verified, and in the case of commuters holding Forms I-151, payroll records were checked to determine the date on which employment commenced and to determine that employment had been continuous. Personnel assigned varied from time to time as the number of workers varied as the labor needs of the farms. The majority of the work was seasonal and varied considerably between seasonal activities.

d. In addition to actions outlined under c above, the Border Patrol force has been augmented during periods of peak activity by details of additional officers. The on-duty force was increased in those areas of greatest activity and an investigative force was detailed into the most active areas to handle investigative matters.

e. District Directors of the respective districts have the responsibility for examining aliens applying for admission to determine their admissibility and to conduct investigations of aliens when it is alleged the alien is in the United States in an illegal status. Chief Patrol Inspectors of the respective sectors of the Border Patrol are responsible for maintaining traffic checking points on roads leading from border areas to intercept illegal aliens and checking aliens employed on farms as to their right to be in the United States.

The entire inspection force at ports of entry is engaged in examining alien applicants for admission. In those areas where it has been certified that labor disputes exist the entire Border Patrol force is engaged in intercepting any illegal alien in transit or employed on a struck farm. The force necessary to investigate aliens allegedly in the United States illegally will vary considerably because of the fluctuation in seasonal agricultural activities. However, sufficient force is assigned such duties in order to keep inspections and investigations current.

f. Checks of struck farms were made by Patrol Inspectors and Service Investigators. During 1968, the six struck farms in Starr County were checked approximately 72 times or an average of each farm once a month. There is no record of the number of persons questioned; however, checks during the period January 25 to October 2, 1968, there were 208 workers questioned including 81 holders of I-151's.

In the Coachella Valley there were 10 farms checked 77 times during the periods June 19–20, 1968, and July 11–18, 1968. There were 544 persons questioned, including 271 holders of Form I-151. During this period there was a restraining order in effect from June 19, 1968, to July 11, 1968.

In calendar year 1969 the 10 farms were checked 136 times and there were 2,542 persons questioned, including 1,655 holders of Form I-151.

g. Struck farms were systematically checked by the Border Patrol. Every resident alien I-151 holder encountered was investigated to determine whether he was in violation of 8 CFR 211.1(b). A thorough and comprehensive investigation was conducted on a priority basis, including verification of residence in the United States, if alleged, or in Mexico. Payroll records (including labor contractors) are checked, school records are checked if school children accompany the alien, and utility records, etc. are checked.

Subcommittee Inquiry

40. With regard to Form I-186, visitors' passes, or the equivalent of said form:

a. How many have been issued to Mexican nationals in each of the last ten years?

b. How many of such passes are outstanding at present?

c. How many of such passes were revoked in each of the past five years? For what reasons?

d. Why isn't the form I-186 issued for a specific term requiring periodic renewal?

e. Why aren't all visitors' dates of entry and departure stamped on a supplementary document, as is now required for visits outside the twenty-five mile border zone?

f. Is the Form I-186 often used as an entry document by persons who subsequently return it to Mexico and proceed beyond the border as illegal entrants?

g. Isn't it true that it is presently impossible to match apprehended illegal entrants with persons who crossed the border using a Form I-186, yet returned the card to Mexico prior to apprehension? If the answer is negative, please provide an explanation.

RESPONSE

a.

BORDER CROSSING CARDS ISSUED IN THE SOUTHWEST REGION:[1]
YEARS ENDED JUNE 30, 1960–1969

Year	Total	Number by I. & N. Service	Number by Consular Offices[2]
Total	2,222,112	1,684,941	537,171
1960	127,579	127,579	
1961	125,800	125,800	
1962	135,560	135,560	
1963	145,194	145,194	
1964	163,372	163,372	
1965	179,065	179,065	
1966	260,570	186,311	74,259
1967	373,948	210,463	163,485
1968	357,394	206,116	151,278
1969	353,630	205,481	148,149

[1] Border Crossing Cards issued by nationality of aliens to whom issued not available.

[2] Consular Offices began issuing border crossing cards in Mexico in August 1965.

b. The Service estimates that as of the end of the fiscal year 1969 there were in actual use 546,000 Forms I-186. It arrived at this figure by subtracting from the number of Forms I-186 issued since the beginning of the program the estimated attrition (deaths, disability, immigration, etc.), the reissuance of Forms I-186, the denials and change of names, and cards voided for cause.

c. Forms I-186 voided:

1965	12,346
1966	24,281
1967	28,347
1968	29,247
1969	31,121

The reason for voiding these documents has not been a reportable requirement. However, the principal grounds for voidance are: violation of the conditions on which the card was issued, discovery after issuance of the existence of grounds of inadmissibility, and alteration and tampering with the card.

d. Until January 10, 1969, the regulations relating to border cross-ing cards provided limitation of validity to a four-year period from date of issuance. Effective January 10, 1969, the regulation was amended to provide validity of such cards until revoked or voided notwithstanding any expiration date which may appear thereon. This change was made because it was concluded that the cost of manpower, if manpower were available, required to reissue cards in regular use, estimated to be in excess of one-half million, could not be justified by the anticipated minimal benefits to be derived from such a program.

e. The question suggests that dates of entry and departure are stamped on a supplementary document in the cases of *all* visitors who proceed outside the 25-mile border zone. No supplementary document (Form I-94, Arrival-Departure Record) showing the date of entry or departure was required for the 39,000,000 Canadian citizens and British residents of Canada crossing the border for tem-porary visits in this country. Similarly, over 89,000,000 nonimmi-grant border crossers were admitted across the Mexican border with-out supplementary documents to show arrival and departure dates.

In view of the tremendous number of nonimmigrant border crossers, which is increasing with each year, the delays in inspection and the traffic backups at border ports if a supplementary document were required to be prepared and stamped for such aliens can read-ily be foreseen. We do not believe the possibility that Mexican non-immigrant border crossers encountered within the 25-mile zone, will remain beyond the 72-hour admission period is serious enough to warrant the issuance of a supplementary document bearing the date of entry. In the cases of Mexican nonimmigrant border crossers who are admitted for more than 72 hours or to proceed beyond the 25-mile limit, the Service does issue a document (Form SW-434 or I-94) which indicates the date to which the alien is authorized to stay.

f. To some extent this is true. Form I-186 holders also occasion-ally mail their cards home in order to prevent their loss. In Service experience this practice has diminished since the change in regula-tions making the I-186 valid only within 25 miles of the border for less than 72 hours unless an additional permit (SW 434) is issued. The Service tries to determine the true means of entry for all aliens claiming entry without inspection. If it is determined that the alien entered with a border crossing card and he does not have the card in his possession when apprehended, efforts are made to recover the I-186 so that it can be voided.

g. It is not impossible to match apprehended illegal entrants with persons who crossed the border using Forms I-186. Applications for Forms I-186 are on file in the Central Office and records of apprehension are sent to the Central Office to determine if an alien claiming entry without inspection had ever made an application for an I-186. This is based on the premise that the alien uses the same name and date and place of birth. This, of course, is not always the case; however, Service officers can very often determine the alien's true name by documents in his possession such as Mexican draft cards, letters, etc.

Subcommittee Inquiry

42. Is it true that at this time holders of Form I-186 are not fingerprinted?

a. Would not fingerprinting bearers of the I-186 facilitate matching the fingerprints of apprehended illegal entrants with I-186 card holders for the purpose of revocation of the card?

b. Isn't it true that this might be undertaken by the Federal Bureau of Investigation as an incident to their national fingerprinting clearing house activities? If the answer is negative, please provide an explanation.

c. Please indicate in detail why a fingerprint is not obtained from visitors.

d. Does the Immigration Service presently intend to institute fingerprinting for the purpose of curtailing abuses of the I-186? If the answer is affirmative, when will such change be effective? If the answer is negative, state the reasons for not using the fingerprint identification.

RESPONSE

After enactment of the Alien Registration Act of 1940 applicants for immigrant and nonimmigrant visas were required to be fingerprinted at U.S. consular offices. Through the years many foreign governments protested this requirement, particularly insofar as it pertained to applicants for nonimmigrant visas. Congress responded to these protests by enacting section 8 of the Act of September 11, 1957, 71 Stat. 641. That statute authorized the Secretary of State and the Attorney General, as a matter of discretion to waive the fingerprint requirement for nonimmigrant visa applicants who were nationals of countries which did not require fingerprinting of United States citizens visiting such countries temporarily. Pursuant to the authority contained in that section, the Secretary of State issued regulations waiving the fingerprint requirement for nonimmigrant visa applicants, 22 CFR 41.116(b).

For some time after the promulgation of those regulations, the Service continued to require fingerprinting of applicants for Mexican Nonimmigrant Border Crossing Cards. In 1965, in an effort to reduce the workload caused by the large number of applicants for visitors' visas at the U.S. consular posts in the interior of Mexico it was agreed by the Department of State and the Service that those consular posts could issue Forms I-186 instead of visitors' visas.

Furthermore, since the Forms I-186 were being issued in place of visitors' visas, and consular officers had not been requiring applicants for nonimmigrant visas to be fingerprinted, consular officers did not require fingerprinting of aliens who applied to them for issuance of Forms I-186. This resulted in the situation whereby an applicant for a Form I-186 was not fingerprinted if he applied at a consulate, but was fingerprinted if he applied at a Service office.

In 1965 the Service initiated a survey to determine whether fingerprint checks of applicants for Form I-186 should be continued. The survey disclosed that in less than 1% of the cases was the check productive of any information not already in Service records. Moreover, the little new information which was obtained was rarely of such significance as to affect the determination of the applications. For example, in four random samplings made between October 1965 and January 1966, which included 13,000 referrals to the FBI during a period of 19 days, every one of the 374 FBI identifications reported contained information already reflected in Service records or of no consequence in the adjudication of the application.

The survey cast a doubt on the practical value served by such checks. The Service requested the views of the Internal Security Division of the Department of Justice as to the desirability or necessity for the checks. After consideration, that Division advised that it would not object to their discontinuance, with the understanding that checks would be required in those instances where the Service officer suspected the alien applicant may have assumed another identity or otherwise concealed an arrest or immigration record.

In consideration of the views expressed by the Internal Security Division and the unproductiveness of these checks, the Service issued instructions to discontinue them except when in the judgment of the adjudicating officer there is reason to believe the fingerprint check might be productive.

The Service has no plans to reinstitute the fingerprinting of Form I-186 applicants for the reasons indicated above.

It should be pointed out that there is usually no difficulty in identifying an apprehended alien if he is in possession of a Form I-186. However, even if Form I-186 holders were fingerprinted, and the fingerprints of an apprehended alien were identified through an FBI check with those of an I-186 holder, there is a very practical difficulty in physically voiding that form if the apprehended alien does not have it in his possession.

Subcommittee Inquiry

44. State the policy of the Service and the Justice Depatrment in detail with reference to waiver of prosecution, and waiver of deportation.

RESPONSE

The Service has no authority to waive prosecution for violation of any of the criminal provisions of the Immigration and Nationality Act. Responsibility for initiating and conducting prosecutions is reposed in the United States Attorneys, under the direction of the Criminal Division of the Department of Justice. The various United States Attorneys issue guidelines as to general or blanket waiver of prosecution for certain criminal violations and the Service abides by these waivers. The United States Attorneys are often influenced in the types of cases prosecuted by the attitudes of the United States District Courts. Past immigration records, family relationship to suspected violators, and various humanitarian aspects are factors considered by United States Attorneys in prosecution cases. Also taken into account are the large number of immigration violations, and the knowledge that the prosecution of all such violations would overburden the courts.

The largest number of cases falling under blanket waiver directions of the United States Attorneys involve illegal entries (8 USC 1325). Generally such cases are not prosecuted unless there are repeated offenses, or where other aggravated factors are present.

Next in volume of cases under blanket waivers are violations of the alien registration provisions of the Immigration and Nationality Act, for which the United States Attorneys seldom authorize prosecution, in the absence of aggravated circumstances.

As a general rule, if an alien returns illegally to the United States after being granted voluntary departure, he is placed under formal deportation proceedings. If he is deported and returns, he is prosecuted under 8 USC 1326 for reentry after deportation, which is a felony.

Waiver of deportation can be effected through a number of remedies provided by statute, such as adjustment of status (sec. 245, 8 USC 1255), registry (sec. 249, 8 USC 1259), and suspension of deportation (sec. 244, 8 USC 1254). Because of statutory limitations some of these remedies are not available to natives of adjacent countries. In addition, deportation may be withheld by the Attorney General if he finds the alien would be subject to persecution on account of race, religion, or political opinion for such period of time as he deems necessary for such reason (sec. 243[h] of the Act, 8 USC 1253[h]). Moreover, the Attorney General has the usual prosecutor's discretion to withhold or terminate deportation proceedings where the infraction was minor, or the consequences would be excessive, or where humanitarian considerations are present.

Probably the Subcommittee's inquiry is concerned more with voluntary departure, which would avert deportation.

Voluntary departure in lieu of deportation is generally granted aliens who were admitted as temporary visitors and later violate status either by remaining longer than permitted or by accepting employment. Voluntary departure is generally granted an illegal entrant who has entered the United States solely to accept employment or where his prior immigration history shows no aggravated immigration offenses. If such an alien reentered illegally after a recent grant of voluntary departure, then deportation proceedings usually are instituted. Taking into account the large volume of illegal entrants across the Mexican border, the Service policy is to grant voluntary departure in these cases. Some 161,000 Mexican aliens were apprehended in fiscal year 1969 after having entered the United States without inspection. It would have been physically impossible to conduct formal deportation proceedings for each such illegal entrants. Therefore, except in aggravated cases, voluntary departure is the only practicable and effective remedy to remove such illegal entrants.

In addition to the voluntary departure granted to natives of foreign contiguous territory, as indicated above, such relief is usually granted to any alien statutorily eligible therefor (1) whose application for extension of stay as a nonimmigrant is being denied; or (2) who has voluntarily surrendered himself to the Service; or (3) who presents a valid travel document and confirmed reservation for transportation out of the United States within 30 days; or (4) who is an F-1, F-2, J-1, or J-2 nonimmigrant and who has lost such status solely because of a private bill introduced in his behalf, or is a J-1 or J-2 nonimmigrant and who has lost such status solely because of the formal filing with the Service of an application for waiver of the two-year foreign-residence requirement; or (5) who is (i) the beneficiary of an approved third-preference petition or (ii) a native of an independent country of the Western Hemisphere or the Canal Zone who has the qualifications of a third-preference alien and has applied for an immigrant visa or (iii) the beneficiary of an approved sixth-preference petition who establishes that he can qualify for third preference, and who cannot obtain a visa solely because a visa number is unavailable, and his child or spouse, including a spouse who is or was a J nonimmigrant and is subject to the foreign-residence requirement; or (6) other than a native or citizen of foreign contiguous territory, who is admissible to the United States as an immigrant, who has a priority date for an immigrant visa not more than 60 days later than the date shown in the latest Visa Office Bulletin, and who has applied for an immigrant visa at an American consulate which has accepted jurisdiction of the case; or (7) in whose case the district director has determined there are compelling factors warranting grant of voluntary departure.

Subcommittee Inquiry

46. Indicate the percentage of formal deportations and prosecutions to apprehensions during the period of Operation Wetback 1953, 1954 and 1955. Is it true that Operation Wetback provided an effective deterrent to subsequent illegal entry for a period of years?

RESPONSE

Years ended June 30, 1953, 1954 and 1955.

Aliens Apprehended 2,229,266
Aliens Deported 61,824
Prosecutions 40,103

Percentage of persons apprehended who were deported or prosecuted was 4.6%.

Operation Wetback, which was in effect between June 17, 1954 and January 1, 1955 was unquestionably a deterrent to subsequent illegal entries. The increase in Border Patrol personnel by some 400 positions in 1955 also was instrumental in stopping illegal entries.

Two major deterrents to illegal entries for the period after January 1, 1955 were:

(1) A workable bracero program for the importation of large numbers of agricultural workers under P.L. 78, 82nd Congress, as amended.

(2) An increase in the number of lawful immigrants from Mexico.

Subcommittee Inquiry

48. Indicate specific plans if any to increase the number of criminal prosecutions and formal deportation proceedings utilizing the new federal magistrate. Reflect a schedule for implementation of such plans.

RESPONSE

Under the new statute, the federal magistrate's trial jurisdiction may be extended to misdemeanors punishable by imprisonment for not more than one year or a fine of not more than $1,000, or both, provided the accused waives trial in the district court. Most immigration offenses now provide for punishment in excess of one year. For example, 18 USC 1546 (falsification or misuse of entry documents) has a maximum punishment of five years; section 276 of the Immigration and Nationality Act, 8 USC 1325 (unlawful reentry after deportation) has a maximum of two years; 18 USC 911 (false claim to United States citizenship) has a maximum of three years; and section 274 of the Immigration and Nationality Act, 8 USC 1324 (smuggling or transporting unlawful entrants) has a maximum of five years. Among the frequent prosecutions, only section 275 of the Immigration and Nationality Act, 8 USC 1325 (unlawful entry), entails maximum punishment under one year. It provides for a maximum of six months and $500 fine for a first offense. For a subsequent commission of such offense, conviction is punished by imprisonment for not more than two years or by a fine of not more than $1,000, or both. Accordingly, only a first offender under section 275 of the Immigration and Nationality Act, 8 USC 1325, could presently be tried before a federal magistrate.

Thus far positions under the Federal Magistrates Act have been established in only five pilot jurisdictions: New Jersey, District of Columbia, Eastern Virginia, Kansas and Southern California. Adverting to the situation in the Southern District of California, which is of primary concern here, there is one full-time magistrate stationed at San Diego and one part-time magistrate at El Centro. Both of these magistrates were appointed on July 1, 1969. Since that date 283 immigration prosecutions were conducted before the magistrate in San Diego and 158 before the magistrate in El Centro. All of these prosecutions have been brought under section 275 of the Immigration and Nationality Act, 8 USC 1325.

As more federal magistrates are appointed and assigned duties by the United States District Courts, more prosecutions can be brought before them. However, the statutory jurisdictional limitations restrict the use of magistrates in immigration cases. Perhaps this difficulty might be overcome by a statute enlarging the jurisdiction of the federal magistrates. However, we do not recommend this approach until the statute has been more fully tested in operation.

Another course might be to seek legislation which would reduce maximum punishment of most, if not all, immigration violations to conform to the jurisdictional limitations of the magistrates. We do not favor such a sweeping diminution of penalties which would require the prosecution of serious violations as minor offenses.

A different approach would involve only the amendment of section 275 of the Immigration and Nationality Act, 8 USC 1325, relating to unlawful entry, by eliminating the distinction between first and second offenders, by increasing the prescribed penalty to a maximum of one year imprisonment and $1,000 fine; and by including attempts to commit the prescribed crimes.

If this change were accomplished, many of the prosecutions presently brought in U.S. District Courts under 18 USC 1546, 8 USC 1326, 18 USC 911 and 8 USC 1324, could be brought before federal magistrates under 8 USC 1325, either because an illegal entry has occurred or because of an attempt to make an illegal entry or because of aiding and abetting the commission of such offense. The desirability of proposing such an amendment is presently being considered.

Subcommittee Inquiry

49. Does the Service have, in the opinion of counsel, the power to levy administrative fines against illegal entrants or persons who harbor or assist illegal entrants?

a. If the answer is negative, indicate from a legal standpoint the grounds underlying that opinion. If the answer is affirmative, indicate the circumstances under which the agency has the power to levy informal administrative fines.

b. Would such power be useful in deterring illegal entrants if monies in their possession were subject to partial confiscation to meet such fines?

RESPONSE

a. The answer is negative in the opinion of counsel. The Immigration and Nationality Act of 1952, 66 Stat. 163, is an organic law within which prescribes all of the powers under the immigration laws granted by Congress to the Attorney General. Section 103(a) of the Act, 8 USC 1103(a), contains the general grant of authority. In pertinent part it provides:

> He shall establish such regulations; prescribe such forms of bond, reports, entries, and other papers; issue such instructions; and perform such other acts as he deems necessary for carrying out his authority under the provisions of this Act.

Many sections of the Act authorize the Attorney General to levy fines administratively for specified violations of law: Act, sections 231, 237, 243, 251, 254, 255, 256, 271, 272 and 273; 8 USC 1221, 1227, 1253, 1281, 1284, 1285, 1286, 1321, 1322 and 1323. Several of the foregoing sections authorize fines for bringing inadmissable aliens to the United States, but none is directed against illegal entrants or those harboring illegal entrants.

It seems clear from the structure of the Act that the legislative intent was to give to the Attorney General express authorization to impose fines in specific situations and to withhold from him the power to impose administrative fines in other situations of his own choosing. A power which has been withheld by Congress cannot be found to exist as an "incidental" or "necessary" power. *Saxon* v. *Georgia Association of Independent Insurance Agents, Inc.*, 399 F.2d 1010 (C.A. 5, 1968). Penal statutes must be construed strictly, so that even if the Act should be deemed ambiguous with regard to the extent of power to impose fines, doubts would have to be resolved against implied authority to impose penalties. 2 Sutherland, *Statutory Construction*, 3rd ed., section 3303; *United States* v. *Minker*, 350 U.S. 179 (1956).

b. The power to impose administrative fines against illegal

entrants would be useful as a deterrent. Service officials advise that they have been seeking for years a sanction more universally applicable than early apprehension as a means of "taking the profit out" of the illegal entrant's enterprise. They advise that until 1968 they considered the feasibility of an administrative fine program, assuming that Congress would authorize it, but reached no conclusion, finding it difficult to resolve doubts whether the benefits of such a program would outweigh administrative complexities and costs as well as delays in expulsion. In particular they perceived the possibility of built-in legal difficulties, recognizing that it is one thing to impose a fine administratively and another to collect it legally against the will of an illegal alien without bringing him before a court or at least giving him the opportunity to sue to keep title to his money. The Service advised that in the end it was decided that more effective approach would be to try to take the fullest advantage of the Federal Magistrates Act of 1968 and to press for sentences including the imposition of fines for violations of criminal laws.

As indicated in our response to Question 48, consideration is being given to the desirability of proposing an amendment to section 275 of the Act, 8 USC 1325, by modifying the prescribed criminal penalties, so as to make the offense of unlawful entry triable before federal magistrates.

Appendix II

THE STORY OF IMMIGRATION

The history of Mexican immigration to the United States is related to the rise of great regional and national industries, i. e., agriculture, railroads, and mining, as well as the corresponding demand for a reservoir of cheap labor; the special administrative and legislative consideration given to immigration from the Western Hemisphere, particularly from Mexico, and the internal developments and changes in Mexico.

1850–1889   Undesirability of Mexicans for labor or settlement corresponded to the importation and utilization of European and Oriental laborers and settlers.

1900–1909   Continued economic development, particularly in the Southwest, and the decrease in the importation and utilization of Oriental labor due to the application and enforcement of the Chinese Exclusion Laws and the Gentleman's Agreement with Japan, led to a moderate increase in the volume of Mexican immigration.

1910–1919   Increased use of Mexican laborers was related to: the decreasing volume of European immigration, World War I mobilization, rise of defense industries, completion of railroads linking the interior of Mexico to the U.S., and the revolutionary conditions in Mexico.

1920–1929   Quotas established. European and Asiatic immigration continued to decrease. Mexican immigration increased, reaching a peak in 1924. Increased restrictions affect immigration which decreases in late 1920's. Illegal Mexican aliens average 4000 per year.

1930–1939   Effects of Great Depression. Mexicans repatriated. Mexican immigration continues to decrease. Illegal Mexican aliens increase and average 10,500 per year. Mexican emigration increases.

1940–1947   World War II. Tremendous increase in demand for labor. U. S. and Mexico make agreement for temporary contract labor (Bracero Program). Illegal Mexican aliens greatly increases. Mexican immigration increases slightly.

1948–1951   Illegals legalized to become Braceros. "Braceros" increase. Mexican immigration remains stable. Public Law 78 enacted. Mexican illegal aliens greatly increase.

1952–1959   Korean War. Demand for labor. Braceros, illegals, and Mexican immigration increase dramatically. Illegal Mexicans constitute a high of 1,075,-168 apprehensions when Operation Wetback inaugurated. Illegals expelled by the thousands.

1960–1970   Bracero Program terminated (1964) due to public pressure. Illegal Mexican aliens on a dramatic increase again. Mexican immigration steadily increasing. New immigration law (Public Law 86-236, passed in 1965, effective July 1, 1968) restricts immigration from Western Hemisphere.

SUMMARY OF MEXICAN MIGRATORY MOVEMENTS TO U.S.*

Type		Period	Total
Mexican immigration	▬▬▬▬▬	1869–present	1,540,000
Temporary contract labor from Mexico	ooooooooooo	1942–present	5,050,000
Illegal Mexican aliens reportedly located	●●●●●●	1924–present	5,630,000**

* Table does not include non-immigrants, i.e., visitors, transients, students.

** Includes duplication where same person located more than once.

Taken from "Map Study of Mexican-Americans," with permission of the publishers, Hearne Brothers. The chart was prepared by Dr. Julian Samora, Jorge A. Bustamante, Gilbert Cardenas, and Carmen Samora.

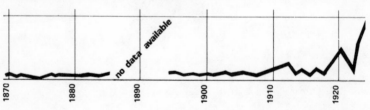

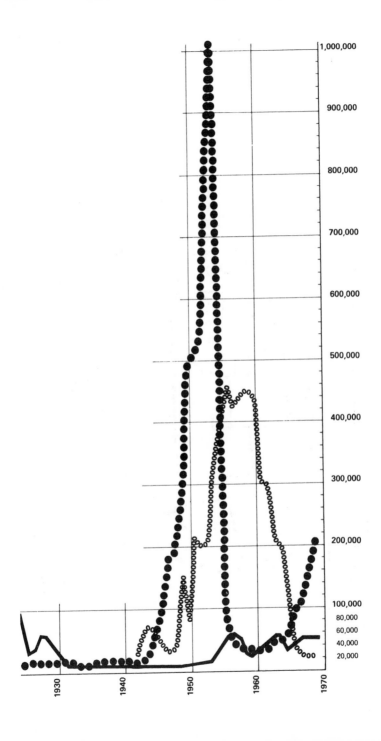

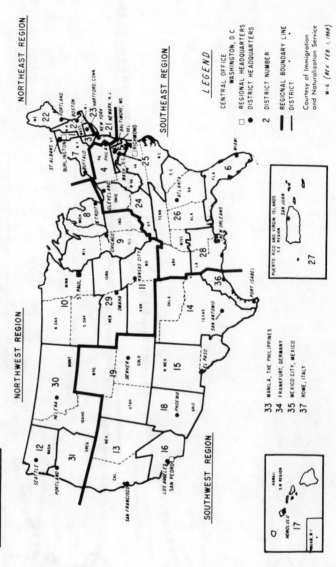

IMMIGRATION AND NATURALIZATION SERVICE
REGIONAL AND DISTRICT AREAS

ALASKA
N W REGION
32

NORTHWEST REGION

NORTHEAST REGION

SOUTHWEST REGION

SOUTHEAST REGION

LEGEND

CENTRAL OFFICE
WASHINGTON, D.C.

□   REGIONAL HEADQUARTERS
●   DISTRICT HEADQUARTERS
2   DISTRICT NUMBER

━━━ REGIONAL BOUNDARY LINE
▎▎▎ DISTRICT

Courtesy of Immigration
and Naturalization Service

M-6 (REV. FEB. 1, 1968)

33 MANILA, THE PHILIPPINES
34 FRANKFURT, GERMANY
35 MEXICO CITY, MEXICO
37 ROME, ITALY

PUERTO RICO AND VIRGIN ISLANDS
S E REGION
SAN JUAN
27

HAWAII
S W REGION
HONOLULU
17

Index

Index